Political Judgment

Key Concepts in Political Theory

Charles Jones and Richard Vernon, *Patriotism*
Roger Griffin, *Fascism*
Peter J. Steinberger, *Political Judgment*

Political Judgment

An Introduction

Peter J. Steinberger

Polity

First published in 2018 by Polity Press

Polity Press
65 Bridge Street
Cambridge CB2 1UR, UK

Polity Press
101 Station Landing
Suite 300
Medford, MA 02155, USA

ISBN-13: 978-1-5095-1310-9 (hardback)
ISBN-13: 978-1-5095-1311-6 (paperback)

A catalogue record for this book is available from the British Library.

Typeset in 10.5 on 12 pt Sabon
by Fakenham Prepress Solutions, Fakenham, Norfolk NR21 8NN
Printed and bound in Great Britain by Clays Ltd, St. Ives PLC

The publisher has used its best endeavors to ensure that the URLs for external websites referred to in this book are correct and active at the time of going to press. However, the publisher has no responsibility for the websites and can make no guarantee that a site will remain live or that the content is or will remain appropriate.

Every effort has been made to trace all copyright holders, but if any have been inadvertently overlooked the publisher will be pleased to include any necessary credits in any subsequent reprint or edition.

For further information on Polity, visit our website:
politybooks.com

For Mo

Contents

Introduction: What is Political Judgment?

In 2012, David Brooks, the *New York Times* commentator, wrote a column about presidential leadership that emphasized, above all, the importance of good judgment. Specifically:

> A president with political judgment has a subtle feel for the texture of his circumstances. He has a feel for where opportunities lie, what will go together and what will never go together. This implicit knowledge is developed slowly in people like Harry Truman or Lyndon Johnson who have spent decades as political insiders and who have a rich repertoire of experiences to draw on.[1]

Its astonishingly gendered language notwithstanding, many or most readers are apt to find this a perfectly intelligible and entirely plausible observation. It seems obvious that the president ought to be an individual of good judgment. The problem, however, is to determine exactly what that is and how it is to be identified in particular individuals. Brooks seems to take a stab at fleshing some of this out. But when he says, for example, that judgment is a matter of having "a subtle feel" and a kind of "implicit knowledge," this seems largely to beg the question. What exactly is such a subtle feel? How is it different from other kinds of mental phenomena? If someone has the requisite implicit knowledge, what exactly does that person know and exactly how does that person know it? To what extent does such knowledge produce judgments that are, in fact, reliable, justifiable, and correct? Is it possible to say with confidence that one particular person has the feel while another one doesn't? In the absence of answers to such questions – without a cogent *theory* of political judgment, a political *philosophy* of judgment – statements like Brooks's seem facile, gratuitous and, in the end, largely useless.

But there are, in fact, theories of political judgment out there, important and serious ones. The topic is, indeed, of long-standing interest – a central theme of political thought – and has been tackled by philosophers of great distinction and influence. It is to an account and analysis of at least some of their theories that this book is devoted.

I begin with an assumption: politics is the process by which communities of people, acting in some kind of collective capacity, decide to pursue certain courses of action and avoid others. It is a matter of making decisions – adopting policies or laws – that have public consequences, in the sense both that they affect lots of people and that they affect those people in their status as citizens of a state. Obviously, political decisions can be made in all kinds of ways. They can be made by autocrats (monarchs, benevolent despots, tyrants), by specific groups of individuals (aristocratic councils, committees of experts, administrative functionaries) or by the larger body of citizens themselves according to any number of possible choice-making procedures (majority rule, unanimity, lottery, and the like). Most theorizing about politics focuses, of course, either on evaluating such various processes against one another or assessing the virtually infinite range of policies and laws that states, using those procedures, have adopted or could adopt in the future. But in all cases, politics is also understood, at least implicitly, to be a matter of judgment. Decisions are not generally made randomly, nor are they made for no good reason at all. They invariably represent at least some effort to judge the relative merits of different options.

The very idea of judgment in politics thus reflects at least two premises, neither of which can plausibly be denied. First, it presupposes that some courses of action – some policies or laws – are better than others. This doesn't mean that there is necessarily one best policy for any given circumstance. It may be difficult or impossible to say with any confidence that a political system, in adopting a particular course of action, has clearly done the single right thing. Nonetheless, we do, and I think must, presuppose that it is generally possible to distinguish between policies that are better and those that are less good. Indeed, the very idea of choosing – of making a decision – assumes that we are able to assess the merits of alternatives in relation to one another and thereby to make sensible choices, that is, to adopt certain courses of action that will be more beneficial than others. Second, all of this presupposes in turn that someone or something – some decision-making entity, whether a single person, a group of people or an institution – has the capacity to adjudicate intelligently among alternatives, to judge their relative virtues; hence somehow to understand and see what will work well and what won't. We assume, in other words, not simply that politics is a matter of judgment, but that good policies are the result of *good* judgment. I believe that there are no significant examples of political action and no significant theories of political endeavor that do not presuppose the importance of, and also the possibility of, developing and identifying the capacity to judge well in politics.

The problem, however, is to determine exactly what that capacity might be. This is, in large part, a conceptual problem. What does it *mean* to have good political judgment? Is it a particular intellectual faculty and, if so, what does it look like? How does it operate and how is it similar to, different from, and connected or not connected with other intellectual faculties? Is political judgment a skill that can be acquired, a body of truth-claims that can be learned, a set of procedures that can be set in motion? Or is it more like an innate attribute? Is it purely practical, or does it have a theoretical foundation? Do certain kinds of people have political judgment?[2] If so, what are their characteristics, and what enables them to judge well? Is political judgment something that can be attributed only to individual persons, or could it be a property of groups of individuals, large or small? If certain people or groups of people do indeed have good judgment, how can that be recognized? How is it possible to decide that this person is a person of good

judgment while that person is not? Is good judgment related
to experience, education, social background, natural ability,
analytic skill, or inexplicable instinct? Is there a connection
between good judgment on the one hand and moral virtue
on the other? Are good judges necessarily good people and
are good people necessarily good judges? Can we, in short,
come up with an account, a philosophical description, a
conceptual definition of political judgment that will allow us
meaningfully to address some or all of these questions? The
problem is obviously of the greatest importance. For if good
politics requires good judgment, then we need to know at
least roughly what we're talking about if we are to pursue
political issues and political action in a reasonably intelligible
and coherent way.

   Our ordinary thoughts about judgment are typically
confused, vague, and unhelpful. Consider what I would
regard as a representative example. In reviewing a book on
the history of the Federal Reserve system in the United States,
Robert Rubin, a former Secretary of the Treasury, writes
as follows: "The Fed's effectiveness ... ultimately depends
on human judgment .... It is true that the Federal Reserve
has sometimes exercised poor judgment. What is clear,
however, is that a number of the reforms currently being
proposed in Congress could undermine the system's effectiveness by adversely affecting the Fed's independence from
Congressional political influence and reducing its policy-
making flexibility."[3] We find here, as we found in the passage
from David Brooks with which this book began, many of the
hallmarks of standard discourse on the subject. Judgment
is thought to be crucial, but there is little or no effort to
describe what it is, how one gets it, how it operates, or how
we recognize it. On the contrary, the implication seems to be
that judgment is almost a kind of mystical property: either
one has it or one doesn't. Rubin's statement implies, further,
that judgment can be the possession of an institution – the
Federal Reserve system itself – rather than of a particular
individual. But elsewhere in his review, Rubin seems explicitly
to connect the good or bad judgment of the system to the
particular qualities of individual persons, namely, various
chairs of the Federal Reserve. There is a clear presupposition
that judgment is not of a piece; it can be good and it can be

bad. But there's virtually no effort at identifying a method, a formula, a set of criteria for distinguishing the one from the other. To be sure, Rubin might well argue that, in this case and perhaps in most or all others, the proof of the pudding is in the eating – which is to say that someone or something has good judgment when the relevant decisions turn out to produce good results. But there are, of course, two problems with this. First, it ignores the possibility that good outcomes might emerge for reasons of luck or other contingent factors, hence despite an absence of good judgment. Surely we believe this to be a not unusual occurrence. And second, waiting until we see the results of decisions is often or even usually too late. We need to have at least some idea as to who does and doesn't have good judgment before decisions are made, hence before the damage, so to speak, has been done. Without this, the idea of good judgment would seem to lose any kind of practical or intellectual force.

Rubin's comments, like those of Brooks, are typical of what we often say and hear about political judgment. Someone is said to be statesmanlike, or to be a shrewd analyst of public affairs, or to have a certain kind of strategic acumen for making good political decisions. Collections of individuals are thought somehow to produce genuine insights, or to have a knack for doing the right thing, or to sense or feel or otherwise intuit the advantages and disadvantages inherent in one course of action versus another. Of course, none of these claims makes any sense without the complementary if often only implicit claim that other people or other groups are somehow deficient in precisely those same terms. Rarely, however, do we encounter serious efforts to unpack, identify, and explain the difference. The presumption seems to be, roughly, that we cannot define good judgment in politics but that we know it when we see it – a presumption that is not only intellectually troubling but also deeply unhelpful as a practical matter, especially in cases where we disagree about who does and doesn't have good judgment – a kind of disagreement that is characteristic, perhaps even constitutive, of politics as we regularly and routinely experience it.

Given all this, it can hardly be surprising that the history of serious political thought – or, at any rate, the history of political philosophy in the West – has sought to address systematically the question of judgment in politics, understood fundamentally as, again, a conceptual problem. The principal goal of the present book is to examine and critically evaluate a number of important approaches that philosophers have thought to be especially promising. Those approaches have been various and often mutually contradictory. Theorists have sharply disagreed – sometimes explicitly, sometimes otherwise – about what it means to have good judgment in politics and how such judgment is to be achieved. But I believe that those disagreements, though persistent, have also been enormously fruitful. They have provided deep insights both into the nature of the problem at hand and into the ways in which we might best understand not simply the question of judgment in politics but the broader question of political right and wrong.

The chapters that follow examine a range of perspectives – from ancient to modern to contemporary – that reflect a fairly wide variety of theoretical, practical, historical and cultural concerns. They deal with a number of very different works that come from very different places and times. In the face of such diversity, however, I propose to put those perspectives in dialogue with one another, thereby embracing a commitment that underlies, I believe, virtually all philosophical and theoretical work, namely, that the pursuit of intellectual problems is a matter of on-going discussion, conversation and discourse that, at one and the same time, embodies and transcends differences of space and time.

1
Foundations: Plato and Aristotle

As with so many other topics of importance in Western political thought, the recognized or canonical discourse of judgment begins largely with Plato. I focus, in particular, on a dialogue from the so-called middle period of Platonic writing, namely, the *Gorgias*. It is true, of course, that scholars have long disagreed about the relationship between the teachings of Socrates on the one hand and those of his most famous pupil, Plato, on the other; and this is perhaps an especially complex problem in a dialogue such as the *Gorgias* where the main character is, as with most of Plato's works, Socrates, but where the central argument is thought in some sense to mark a certain kind of transition from the Socratic to the Platonic. Given the focus of the present book, however, it is also a problem that we can largely ignore. For what is of interest to us is simply the doctrine of judgment that one finds in the work. As a matter of convenience, then, I intend simply to assume that the doctrine in question is Plato's, which is hardly an eccentric claim; and so it is with Plato, I suggest, that we find a canonical and enormously influential statement of the idea that judgment in politics is essentially a matter of *rationality*. The faculty of rational thought, broadly conceived, is the best or perhaps only reliable and intelligible source of good judgment in politics – a proposition that turns out to have wide-ranging implications both for theorizing about political society and for the actual practice of politics.

1

The *Gorgias* ostensibly presents a discussion between Socrates and the title character, a famous sophist widely celebrated for his intellectual prowess and accomplishment. In fact, it turns out that Gorgias is not so clearly the main interlocutor of the dialogue, or at least not the only significant one, for his role as opponent to Socrates is quickly taken up by two colleagues, Polus and Callicles, each of whom has important things to say on a variety of issues. With respect to judgment, however, the opening discussion with Gorgias is, perhaps, particularly important and revealing. Indeed, it presents what is, I would suggest, a foundational set of claims regarding exactly what it means to talk about judgment in politics.

Socrates begins by asking Gorgias to explain what he does – which is to say that he inquires as to Gorgias's profession. Gorgias responds by saying that he is a rhetorician and that he is, as such, skilled both in the practice of rhetoric and in teaching that practice to others. The ensuing exchange is a prototypical example of the Socratic method or *elenchus*, a Greek word meaning, roughly, refutation. Socrates asks Gorgias to describe the practice of rhetoric – what does it mean to be a rhetorician – and Gorgias answers by indicating, plausibly enough, that to be good at rhetoric is to be good at using words.[1] Of course, there are a great many human activities – arguably most – that in one way or another involve the use of words. Doctors use words to talk about disease and treatment, builders use words to communicate plans and work schedules, military leaders use words to formulate tactics and strategies, and so on. Does Gorgias mean, therefore, that every one of those activities is basically a matter of rhetoric and that he himself is an expert in all of them? Such a suggestion would be plainly absurd, and Gorgias clarifies: a rhetorician is someone who is skilled at using words *apart from* or *independently of* any particular manual endeavor. It is a matter of words and words alone.

Good doctors use rhetoric to communicate effectively with their patients, but this is only one small part of what it means to be a good doctor. A professional rhetorician, on the other hand, is primarily or solely concerned with the effective use of language. This is another plausible qualification of the initial claim. It appears to comport with our ordinary intuitions about what it means to be skilled in rhetoric. Socrates points out, however, that while things like medicine and building and military command are not just about words, a fairly wide variety of other, seemingly quite different activities are, or at least appear to be. He mentions arithmetic and calculation, geometry and chess. That's an interesting collection of examples, not obviously parallel to one another, but it does seem true that each of them involves little or no physical activity; rather, they are all primarily matters of thought itself, and presumably the thoughts are, in each case, part and parcel of the words that are used to express them. Does Gorgias want to say, then, that mathematics – which seems to be a purely verbal activity – is basically rhetoric? Once again, such a claim would be unlikely, to say the least; but how then does rhetoric differ from mathematics, and from many of those other things that are primarily linguistic? Here Gorgias changes direction slightly. He now indicates that rhetoric is not simply about using words. It is, rather, a particular and distinctive way of using words. Specifically, it is the activity of deploying words in order to convince others to believe something that they might not otherwise believe. It is the art of persuasion. Again, it is a plausible suggestion, but again Socrates is not satisfied. An arithmetician uses words to teach arithmetic, and this means using words to persuade students that certain things are arithmetically correct and others not. Is that what Gorgias has in mind? More specifically, does the rhetorician try to demonstrate or prove to his or her listeners what is *true*, as the teacher of arithmetic does, or is the goal rather to get the audience to believe one thing rather than another, *regardless* of whether or not it is actually true? Is the goal, in short, to produce knowledge or is it to produce beliefs that might or might not be matters of knowledge?

Gorgias's response to this last challenge is difficult and equivocal, and it is here that other individuals – Polus and

Callicles – begin to jump into the conversation. They do so by asking Socrates what *he* thinks rhetoric is, and his response is, arguably, the central claim of the entire dialogue: rhetoric is a kind of "knack."[2] The Greek word he uses is *empeiria*. This could also be translated as "experience" or "habitude," and it is precisely in the complexity or subtlety of translation that we may find any number of clues as to what Plato, speaking in the voice of Socrates, has in mind. Consider, to begin with, the activity of playing a flute, which Plato regards as a typical example of a knack. We would all agree that some people play the flute very well, others much less so. But how shall we explain the difference? Plato seems to identify two factors. On the one hand, certain individuals simply have more talent for the flute than others. They have, as we say, natural gifts; and indeed, it is a long-standing feature of our understanding of the world that gifts of this kind are not equally shared. For many or most areas of human endeavor, some people are talented, others not so much; and with respect to flute playing, this means that some simply have a special knack for doing it well. On the other hand, we also realize that our talents, such as they may be, can be exploited more or less assiduously. Mere natural ability, however real, is often not enough; whatever the activity, even the most talented among us usually have to work at it. In the case of the flute, then, a serious, perhaps even monomaniacal dedication to conscientious and diligent practice – the constant, recurrent, habitual effort to develop ever more dexterity in the fingers and an ever more symmetrical embouchure – becomes a necessary condition for being able truly to develop the knack. But notice what this means. The expert flute player is, for two different reasons, unable to provide an *account* of what he or she is doing. The activity in question is not the product of systematic rational and theoretical self-reflection. It is not underwritten by any kind of analysis. Rather, it is a result, first, of sheer, innate, inexplicable ability as developed and perfected through, second, a training regimen – involving, often, a program of endless repetition – that constitutes, in and of itself, a significant level of "experience" and that, as such, gives rise to an appropriate "habitude." The more we work at it, the more our fingers and lips are apt to do what they're supposed to. The improvement in our innate facility seems not to be the result of a self-conscious explanatory or theoretical mode of thinking. It is not an abstract, intellectual process. It is, rather, a matter of habituation. Exactly how does this occur? How is it that we can develop the appropriate muscle memory? What explains the fact that practice makes perfect? Ordinarily, we don't really know, especially if we're not experts in bio-mechanics. We know only that things usually get better through repeated effort, that hard work often pays off. It is true, of course, that we sometimes devise methods or routines that seem to increase the effectiveness of our training efforts and that can be codified as general rules. But such rules are apt to be largely heuristic in nature, prescribing, for example, standard exercises that have proven over time to be successful for reasons that nonetheless remain unclear, unknown and perhaps unknowable. The result is, again, a knack – something that might be very reliable but that cannot give a systematic explication or account of itself.

It is true, of course, that excellent flute playing appears to be not simply a matter of technical expertise or dexterity. Technical control is a perhaps necessary but certainly far from sufficient condition; for great flute playing involves, above all, a kind of interpretive or expressive ability or insight that allows the artist to capture the deepest and most aesthetically satisfying features of whatever music is being played and to provide his or her listeners with as much musical pleasure as possible. Here, presumably, is where we find the real gift of the virtuoso. But it seems likely that this crucial aspect of excellent musicianship also defies any kind of formal analysis involving rules, principles, or causal mechanisms. It may well be that practice helps, and it seems likely that a musician who has a lot of experience in pleasing audiences will, because of that experience, be more adept in continuing to please them. But exactly how and why this occurs remains unclear. There is, it seems, no algorithm, methodology, or formal rational system that can reliably account for the beauty or sublimity of a musical performance. Artistic achievement of this kind evidently reflects a type of knack – something inarticulable, ineffable and, as such, beneath, or perhaps above, analysis.

Plato provides other examples of knacks, and the case of culinary art – the activity of producing fine cuisine – may be especially revealing. As with flute playing, there seems to be no step-by-step methodology for creating innovative, inspired, and delicious food. The master chef, unlike the ordinary cook, has, as we say, a certain *je ne sais quoi*, something that far transcends anything that one might find in a standard cookbook. But the example of cookery also helps bring to light certain aspects of Plato's formulation that are perhaps not immediately apparent in the case of flute playing but that are extremely important for our consideration of judgment. Plato takes pains to differentiate sharply the culinary art from that of medicine. These two activities are similar in that both are devoted to taking care of the body. But whereas the former seeks to provide a certain kind of physical gratification by producing dishes that taste good, the latter aims to address real physical needs by, among other things, prescribing diets that are good for you. Delicious is one thing, nutritious quite another; and Plato indicates that while it is impossible to provide an account – an analysis, causal theory, set of rules – that explains why certain things please the palette more than others, some such account is, at least in principle, readily available with respect to nutrition. Far from being a knack, the science of medicine in general, and nutrition science in particular, is science indeed. It invokes systematic, evidence-based arguments about foods, bodies, and the relationships between them that are designed to demonstrate or to prove why it is that some foods are healthier than others. This is certainly not to say that doctors always get it right. Nutrition science, like all science without exception, is subject to revision, and sometimes the revision is radical in the extreme. Indeed, the very idea of science is to prove the truth of things, while at the same time recognizing that virtually every proof is apt to be overturned or qualified as science continues to progress. Nutrition science is certainly no exception. But, like all of the sciences, it is driven – in large part, constituted – by the ambition to prove objectively the claims that it makes. For a master chef to embrace such an ambition, on the other hand, would be silly, incoherent, a kind of category mistake. So too for the flute playing virtuoso, and for any other practitioner of what Plato calls a knack. Things of that nature do not admit of proof.

Rhetoric is, according to Plato's *Gorgias*, yet another example of a knack, and it is, as such, to be distinguished sharply from what Plato regards as its natural counterpart, namely, politics. Just as cookery and medicine are both devoted to the care of the physical body, so rhetoric and politics are both devoted to justice, morality, and what Plato calls the good of the soul, by which he means, approximately, addressing questions about how best to lead one's life, both individually and in concert with others. And just as cookery and medicine are quite different, so too for rhetoric and politics. Indeed, we might say that rhetoric is to politics very much as cookery is to medicine; and such a comparison helps us see a feature of knack-based activity that has thus far been only implicit. Plato argues – through the character of Socrates, of course – that knacks, without exception, have as their goal the satisfaction of one or another kind of desire. The flute player seeks to create music that will charm or please or otherwise beguile the audience. The master chef seeks to prepare dishes that will fulfill the yearning of diners – their lust – for food that tastes good. And the rhetorician, according to Plato, seeks to employ words that his or her listeners and readers will enjoy, in the sense of finding them beautiful, comforting, persuasive, inspiring, moving, entertaining or otherwise appealing. As we have seen, there is no possibility of really knowing what it is that makes knacks such as these successful. In each case, the knack reflects some kind of inexplicable gift, as perfected somehow through practice and experience. But Plato wants to suggest that at least part of the reason for this is that there is, as we say, no accounting for taste. Who knows how and why the audience at a concert will be charmed, or which dishes the patrons at a restaurant will prefer, or why some speeches seem to be more effective than others? Some people will be moved to tears by a Mozart flute concerto or, perhaps, by Rampal's interpretation of it, whereas others will be bored to tears or will find Rampal's version unappealing or even ugly. One diner may adore the duck liver while another finds it disgusting. You might react with enthusiasm to the candidate's speech while your friend reacts with indifference or contempt. The problem is that all such things seem to be matters of merely subjective preference or taste. There appears to be no rule, algorithm, system, or method for appealing to the ears or palettes or political prejudices of audiences, no step-by-step procedure that will ensure success and/or account for that success, no science of cause and effect that might explain who and how many will like what. In order to be successful, the practitioner of flute playing or cookery or rhetoric has to rely on something else – an instinct, a sense or feel for what will work, an inexplicable intuition.

The case of medicine is, for this very reason, entirely different. As we have seen, the goal of medicine is good health. But while a healthy person will almost certainly feel just fine, good health is not simply or primarily a matter of how a person feels. It is a matter of how well the body functions, and there are clear, identifiable criteria for determining that. We don't know objectively what a delicious meal is, but we do know objectively what a healthy body is; and it is precisely for this reason that the doctor has, at least in principle, an opportunity (though also an obligation) to discover or develop the rules, theories, procedures, and analyses that explain how it is that a certain kind of diet will help produce a properly functioning human organism. While the chef, like the flute player, is lacking in any kind of systematic, rational knowledge of how to produce the intended result, hence has to rely on a mere knack in order to gratify desires or tastes or preferences that are themselves irrational and inexplicable, the doctor's expertise is based precisely on a systematic, scientific understanding of the body. That's what differentiates a doctor from a "quack."

It is with this analysis in mind that Plato proposes a definition of politics and, relatedly, of what it means to have political judgment. If rhetoric is like flute playing and cookery in aiming to fulfill someone's desire but in being unable to explain how it succeeds or fails at least in part because desires themselves are fickle, irrational, subjective, and irrational, the activity of politics, like medicine, is a profoundly rational, even scientific enterprise that operates on the basis of evidence, proof, and rational belief. Just as the doctor aims for the good health of the body, so the politician – the *true* politician – aims for the good health of the body politic, that is, the community, the polis, the society, the state. Just as the doctor knows what a healthy body is, so does the politician know what a healthy political state is. And just as the doctor understands how and why certain kinds of dietary habits are more conducive to good health than others, so does the politician know how and why certain laws or policies or other acts of government will contribute positively to the well being of the body politic. For Plato, then, politics is not at all a matter of *empeiria* – not a knack, an experience, or a habitude. It is, rather, a *technē*, a Greek word from which we derive such English words as technology. *Technē* is often translated as "craft" or "art." Plato's use of it, however, suggests something much closer to what we call science.

In thinking of political judgment as a *technē*, Plato effectively inaugurates the rationalist tradition of Western political thought. The upshot of his account is to be found not primarily in the *Gorgias* but in his most widely read work, the *Republic*, where he insists on the rational, scientific nature of political activity and political judgment, properly understood. As with the *Gorgias*, Plato's ideas in the *Republic* are expressed through the character of Socrates, who is engaged in a long conversation with several interlocutors about the meaning of the concept of justice; and the first part of the dialogue is famously devoted to a systematic description of an ideal state, the so-called *kallipolis* or "beautiful city," composed of several classes of individuals who are expected to perform only those functions for which they are naturally suited and governed by a special class of guardians. While the account of the ideal state is arguably what most people think of when they think about the *Republic*, many readers, including many quite accomplished ones, have failed to notice that in the middle of Book 5, exactly half-way through the work and after the *kallipolis* has been described in great detail, the topic changes dramatically.[3] Rather than continuing to present and analyze an ideal political society, Socrates suddenly addresses a brand new and quite different question: what would be the easiest way to reform real, existing cities – presumably cities like Athens and Sparta, among others – so that they might become as well governed as possible.[4] It is there that we encounter what is almost certainly the most notorious claim of Platonic political thought: the best way to improve the government of any particular political society would be to make sure that the rulers are philosophers and the philosophers rulers.

This is an inflammatory and highly controversial proposition and it has several important implications. First, it reflects a profoundly undemocratic or even anti-democratic perspective. Plato is clear that philosophy is not for everyone. Only the few can aspire to philosophical knowledge, a kind of knowledge that presupposes both extraordinary and unusual intellectual talent and perhaps equally extraordinary and unusual virtues of character. Philosophers are very smart, indeed the smartest among us. But they are also persons of exceptional moderation and self-control, either uninterested in the kinds of pleasures, entertainments, and other distractions with which most of us are preoccupied, or else quite able to control and regulate any desire that they might have for such things. Moreover, the training of the philosophers is an education precisely in systematic, rational inquiry that has, as its principal aim, the discovery of true propositions about how things in the world really are. In the terms that we have been using, philosophy is indeed a *technē*, a matter of reliable, scientific truth; and Plato's emphasis on the political relevance of philosophy – indeed, his insistence that political authority should be placed in the hands of those with philosophical knowledge and a philosophical temperament – presupposes, among other things, that in politics there is always a fact of the matter to be discovered. Just as the doctor has access to a wide range of facts that really do determine both what a healthy body is and what kinds of things cause a body to be healthy, so does the philosopher/king – the ruler – have access to an at least equally wide range of facts that describe the justice of a political system and that explain how such a system is to be achieved and maintained. Of course, in achieving and maintaining justice, the philosopher/king will have to make lots and lots of decisions. He or she will have to exercise judgment; and Plato's central claim is that, in such a circumstance, the exercise of judgment is not a knack at all. It is not some mysterious, ill-defined talent, not a matter of mere intuition, feeling, or instinct. Unlike such things as flute playing and cookery – and, most important, unlike rhetoric – it is not a matter of what Socrates, in the *Gorgias*, calls "shrewd guessing."[5] There is, in the well-governed state, no guesswork at all. We are dealing here with a precise, rigorous, fact-based manner of thought. The philosopher/king knows what the right thing to do is, and can explain exactly why it is the right thing to do. He or she can give a systematic account of his or her decisions, meaning that he or she can adduce evidence and reasons that will demonstrate why those decisions are the correct ones. The philosopher/king is a kind of expert, but it is an expertise that invokes, if need be, an elaborate structure of explanatory justification. "This," says the ruler of the well-governed society, "is the right thing to do and I can prove it."

Such a theory may seem shocking and unattractive. As indicated above, it is plainly and deeply elitist and profoundly hostile to any plausible notion of democracy. But consider the alternative. Do we want political decisions – involving matters of, say, war and peace, the basic distribution of goods and services in society, law and punishment, fundamental rights and freedoms, justice and welfare – to be decided by someone or something that has little more than an indefinable, ineffable, elusive knack? Should political society be driven primarily by the passing whims, desires, and irrational preferences or prejudices of a population that might have neither the time nor the ability or knowledge to think about complicated issues in a serious and comprehensive manner? Do we want policies to reflect the power of rhetoric, a power that, as history amply shows, can be misused to terrible effect? Should we put our fate in the hands of individuals whose abilities and dispositions are, in some non-trivial sense, mysterious, arcane, and nebulous? These are the kinds of concerns that almost certainly motivated Plato to formulate his craft-theory of political rule, a theory that ultimately reduces to the simple, seemingly straightforward proposition that political authority ought to be in the hands of those individuals who are not only devoted to the common good but who, at the same time, know what they're doing. This is, in effect, a plea both for competence and for ensuring that there are methods and procedures for assessing who is and who isn't competent.

I would suggest that Plato offers what might be called a baseline conception of political judgment. It puts a premium on considerations of knowledge and rationality. It argues that in politics, as in many or most other things, there are right and wrong answers, or at least answers that are demonstrably better than other answers. And it suggests that discovering those better answers is not a haphazard business but reflects, quite on the contrary, a systematic, orderly and evidence-based process rooted in fundamental conceptions of what it means to be a rational human being.

2

A standard objection to the Platonic approach pertains to its feasibility. If it is difficult to identify reliably the truly skilled flute player, chef, or rhetorician, wouldn't it be even more difficult to identify those who have the kind of philosophical knowledge appropriate for politics, and difficult, as well, to arrive at a process for ensuring that such people, if we could find them, are actually put in positions of authority? Plato himself recognizes the problem, and views it as a kind of paradox: how could those with knowledge and ability convince those without knowledge and ability – presumably the vast majority of us – that philosophers should rule?[6] Wouldn't such a decision presuppose the existence of a citizen-body that has exactly the kind of theoretical sophistication that citizen-bodies in fact lack, which is why they need to be ruled by philosophers in the first place? It is a difficult problem, but not self-evidently irresolvable. After all, in ordinary life we regularly and routinely rely on people who are experts, even though we are not experts ourselves; and in so doing, we very often have clear, agreed-upon procedures for determining who the real experts are. We make sure that our brain surgeons have the craft of brain surgery, that our engineers have the scientific knowledge to build bridges that won't collapse, that our automobile mechanics understand how cars work and how they can be fixed; and so too for dozens of other craft-based activities. In most such cases, societies have adopted and endorsed training protocols that provide the requisite knowledge, reliable and widely accepted tests, or other criteria that certify whether or not an individual has actually mastered the relevant *technē*, and on-going systems of evaluation to ensure that the work is being done properly. Indeed, the world we live in is virtually unthinkable without the belief that it is possible to discover, develop, and rely upon all manner of experts who know what they're doing, and whose knowledge is not merely a knack of some kind but reflects, rather, a more or less explicit and discursive understanding of how things in the world – not all things, but at least some important ones – actually work. If, the Platonist asks, we can do this for things like brain surgery, engineering, and automobile repair, why not also for politics?

Two other objections, however, are less easily dismissed. While Plato disparages knacks in the harshest terms – again, anyone who has a knack has, in effect, no knowledge whatsoever – he nonetheless implicitly recognizes what we all know, namely, that some people can perform knack-like activities with considerable reliability. The skilled flute player really is good at what he or she does, as is the accomplished chef, the expert rhetorician, and many other practitioners of *empeiria*; and the possession of such skills seems not to be merely accidental. If it is true, moreover, that there's no accounting for taste and that the flute player's interpretation, like the chef's creation or the rhetorician's words, will please some people and not others, it seems also true that some practitioners are particularly adept at winning over extremely large audiences. They are somehow in touch with, as we say, the pulse of the people. Again, a knack, including the ability to gratify the desires of very many customers, can be learned; and if learning comes more easily to those with natural talent, it is also often quite possible to identify students who do indeed have special abilities. Something real, something concrete, is going on here. We want to say that the virtuoso knows what he or she is doing, and this seems directly to belie Plato's claim that such people know nothing.

It is also the case, moreover, that many of the activities associated with and indeed characteristic of politics seem not well suited to the strictures of Platonic science, or any other science, for that matter. A political executive – say, the President of the United States – has to select someone to be a cabinet officer. A legislator has to decide whether to support or oppose a proposed policy on health-care or crime or the budget. A voter will have to choose among candidates for public office. An appeals court judge has to interpret a complex and arcane constitutional provision. A diplomat must discover the best way to pursue a delicate negotiation.

A bureaucrat must apply a rule in circumstances where it is not obvious how to do it. A juror must assess the guilt or innocence of a defendant. The political system as a whole will adopt strategies for identifying, conceptualizing, and addressing an enormous range of issues having all manner of moral, social, economic, military, ideological, and legal implications. These are prototypically matters of political judgment, and they do not seem to be the kinds of things that can be decided scientifically. Our intuition is that they are, indeed, matters of skill and, as such, seem more akin to such things as flute playing, cookery, and rhetoric. And yet, at the same time, we are apt to resist the notion that they are mere knacks, lacking any kind of rule-governed, knowledge-based, rationally discoverable and demonstrable principles, standards, or criteria. Our sense is that political judgment is more than mere luck, more than simply a hit-or-miss enterprise, more than an ineffable, non-rational, elusive type of endeavor, the foundations of which remain mysterious. But clearly we have a problem. For if political judgment is neither scientific nor magical, neither a *technē* nor an *empeiria*, neither strictly rational nor purely aesthetic, then what exactly is it?

This, precisely, is the question that Aristotle explicitly raises and seeks to resolve. In doing so, he actually initiates what has been called the "judgment tradition" of Western political thought. It is a tradition – alive and well today – that emphatically rejects Platonic science, or any standard form of scientific or philosophical rationalism, as a way of thinking about prudence or political wisdom in politics but that pursues, nonetheless, the exceedingly challenging and often frustrating project of positing or discovering a compelling alternative account that can make sense of judgment in politics, understood as an enterprise that is, despite being un-Platonic, profoundly rationalistic.

For Aristotle, all human intellectual activity is governed by standards of "right reason" in order to "hit a target." By right reason, he simply means a reliable manner of thinking, the reliability of which can be explained through some kind of analysis; by hitting a target, he means finding the correct solution to a particular problem. But in Aristotle's view, we encounter different kinds of problems in life, and finding the correct answer requires appropriately different modes of thinking. There are, in fact, no less than three different kinds of right reason, depending on the type of problem we're trying to solve.

One problem – or "target" – is to understand how things in the world really are. This means nothing other than discovering what the world is composed of and how the world works. It is a matter of describing and understanding reality and, as such, seeks to distinguish what is true from what is false. For Aristotle, this is the domain of *theōria* or theoretical wisdom, by which he means, roughly, science, if we include in science not only things like biology, chemistry, and physics but also mathematics and other forms of reasoned analysis. In Aristotle's view, science is concerned only and exclusively with matters "that cannot be other than they are." This is to say that, in investigating reality, we seek to understand the unchanging truth of things. If we discover, say, that the internal angles of a triangle always add up to one hundred and eighty degrees, neither more nor less, we are discovering a fact about the world that, as far as we can tell, has always been true and will always be true, whether or not it is explicitly known. Triangles are what they are, independent of us; our goal is not to invent the facts about triangles but to discover them. We have, so to speak, no freedom in the matter. Similarly, if we find that every molecule of water is necessarily composed of two hydrogen atoms and one oxygen atom, we are saying that we have discovered something about reality. Water just is, and will always be, two parts hydrogen and one part oxygen. This it not to say that we always get things right. Indeed, science is constantly changing and, in the process, correcting its previous limitations and errors. But Aristotle's point is that reality itself – including those parts of reality that move or evolve or otherwise transform themselves – is what it is, regardless of our wishes and regardless of our point of view. The world operates according to unchanging laws – the kinds of laws that, for example, Galileo or Newton or Einstein would seek to discover. Those laws describe things as they actually are.

Importantly, Aristotle's view is that the kind of right reason that is suited to finding the laws of nature – and, therefore, suited to "hitting the target" of establishing scientific truth – involves a combination of deduction and induction. Deduction is a matter of thinking logically, and this requires what Aristotle calls the faculty of *nous*. The word itself is difficult to translate and has been rendered in many different ways, but we can say that it refers roughly to our capacity to intuit and understand certain fundamental principles of thought, including the basic principles of rational inference. These are principles that cannot be proven or demonstrated, since proof or demonstration presupposes them. Either you "see" them or you don't; and seeing them is necessary for doing science. But science also requires the faculty of *epistēmē* – "science" in a more narrow or specific sense. This involves our capacity to perceive categories of things accurately with our senses – empirically to distinguish red things from blue things, big things from small things, hard things from soft things, and so on, and to discover connections, primarily causal connections, among the various categories of things that we observe. Together, *nous* and *epistēmē* allow us to produce logical, systematic accounts of those connections. Such accounts must be both true to our observations and rationally coherent so that we can deduce from them a system of natural laws that correctly describe how the world works. The full set of such laws – the product of *nous* plus *epistēmē* in tandem – would constitute scientific truth or *thēōria*.

A very different set of problems involves questions not of how things in the world really are but, rather, what kinds of things we should do. Here we are concerned with matters that, so to speak, might have been other than they are. I went out for Chinese food last night, but I could have gone out for steak instead. I decide to become a political philosopher, but I could have decided to become a plumber or a dentist or a drug dealer. I voted for the Socialist candidate, but I could have voted Libertarian. In all such cases, we are talking about making choices, and the "target" we're trying to hit – the goal – is to choose well. For Aristotle, this is not primarily a matter of *thēōria* or theoretical wisdom. It requires, rather, a very different kind of right reason – a type of intellectual approach or manner of thinking that will help us choose the best course of action. Aristotle calls this *phronēsis*, which we can translate as practical wisdom, prudence, or judgment. Good judgment is, for Aristotle, the capacity to choose well when one has choices to make. Whereas *theōria* or science is a matter of affirming or denying claims about how things in the world really are, *phronēsis* or judgment is a matter of pursuing or avoiding outcomes by acting one way rather than another.

As indicated above, Aristotle identifies a third kind of intellectual virtue or right reason, namely, *technē* or craft. We have seen that Plato believes political judgment precisely to be a kind of *technē*, but Aristotle uses the word in a very different way. For Aristotle, *technē* is always a matter of making things: chairs, houses, automobiles, works of art, and the like. It is devoted to *poēisis*, or production. Like *phronēsis*, it is concerned with things that might have been other than they are. The carpenter made a chair but might have made a desk; he made a red chair but might have made a blue one; he made it out of wood but might have made it out of iron. *Technē* is thus, like judgment, a matter of choosing well. But unlike judgment, the focus is not on choosing an *action* for itself – a mode of behavior, a way of life. The focus, rather, is on the *product*. One might say that it doesn't matter how you build a chair as long as you do whatever is required to build a good one.

For some purposes, Aristotle's concept of *technē* is of the highest importance. But for our purposes, we can ignore it and concentrate on the difference between *theōria* and *phronēsis*. If *theōria*, which aims at uncovering reality, is composed of *nous* (intuitive knowledge of basic principles) and *epistēmē* (causal, empirical science), *phronēsis*, which aims at choosing the right course of action, is composed of *nous* plus *aretē* or moral virtue. Here Aristotle uses *nous* in a somewhat different sense to refer to our ability to see the special, distinguishing features of particular things. *Nous*, for example, allows us to recognize faces. This is something we do all the time, with great reliability. But how do we do it? Aristotle wants to say that our ability to recognize faces and other particular things is, like our ability to grasp fundamental principles of thought, a matter not of proof or argument but of immediate insight or intuition. Again, either you see it or you don't. Judgment or *phronēsis* thus requires the capacity simply to perceive the best course of action given the circumstances. But such a capacity is not enough. One must also have moral virtue, which is, for Aristotle, a kind of correct desire. Specifically, it is the desire to achieve a happy, healthy, productive, thriving kind of life, which is the best life of all. It is the desire to be a good person. If an individual understands through *nous* what is the best course of action but is corrupted by immoral, unvirtuous passions or impulses – greed, excessive lust, pride, envy – then he or she will not be practically wise, will not be a person of good judgment, hence will not choose well. *Phronēsis* requires both insight into the nature of particular things and a commitment to ethical living.

But exactly how does good judgment operate? What does the person of good judgment actually do, or how does he or she actually think? What are the relevant thought processes? In Aristotle's view, *phronēsis* is above all a matter of deliberation. Before choosing a particular course of action – for example, Chinese food rather than steak – we consider the alternatives. We assess advantages and disadvantages, evaluate possible outcomes, attempt to identify unintended consequences, calculate possibilities. Now in emphasizing deliberation – the weighing of pluses and minuses, costs and benefits – Aristotle certainly seems to be on to something. But how do we actually do it? How does deliberation take place, and how do we distinguish good deliberation from bad? If our deliberations are not matters of *theōria* – not science – but of *phronēsis* or prudence, how exactly does this work? To put the issue perhaps most succinctly: if right reason in science is, as we have seen, a matter of deduction and induction, and if judgment is not scientific, then what kind of right reasoning does the person of judgment employ?

This, ultimately, is the basic question for all theories of judgment, political or otherwise. What kind of reasoning – what mental process – is involved in judgment, and how are good judgments therefore justified? How do we know that they're good? Aristotle's answer is both provocative and deeply unsatisfying. As we have seen, judgment is informed by insight into the character of particular things (*nous*) and is guided by moral virtue (*aretē*). To this Aristotle adds the idea that the person of good judgment must be a person of moderation or temperance, able to control his or her passions and impulses. Moderation helps assure that the individual's desires will be correct, that he or she will want the right things. Beyond that, *phronēsis* also involves something called *sunēsis*, which is, roughly, the ability accurately to attach general concepts to particular things, to say, for example, that the small, brown furry thing over there and the much larger, black, less furry thing over here are both dogs, despite their apparent differences. It requires, as well, the virtue of *gnōmē*, which seems to mean something like good old-fashioned common sense, especially with respect to notions of fairness and equity. But Aristotle says very little about how these various things actually operate or how we know whether or not they're working well. Who is to say, for example, what common sense is? What kind of intellectual activity guarantees or even conduces to choosing well? Plato had insisted that good judgment is a rational activity in the sense that it can give an account – an argument, proof, demonstration, justification – in support of its conclusions. Again, Aristotle both denies that judgment is scientific and nonetheless insists that it is not a mere knack, not a matter of shrewd guessing. It is some third thing – a kind of "correctness in reasoning" and a "truthful characteristic of rational choice." But as far as I can tell, he utterly fails to indicate exactly where we find its correctness, exactly what is the source of its truthfulness, exactly how it functions as a form of rationality.

Aristotle is very clear about what judgment is not. It does not produce the kind of rational truth that theoria seeks to generate. It produces a different kind of rational truth. But Aristotle's positive account of this is, at once, evocative and frustratingly imprecise. Is there a manner of thinking, a mode of knowledge, a type of right reasoning that is neither science nor knack, that is less certain and rigorous that what we demand of biologists or chemists, physicists or mathematicians, but that is, at the same time, more concrete and reason-based than what we find in things like flute playing, cookery or rhetoric? Interestingly this is the very question with which Aristotle began. It is, moreover, a question that he reformulates in ways that deepen and enrich our grasp of the relevant issues; his discussion of these issues is suggestive, intriguing, even inspiring. Yet, for all that, the question remains largely unanswered. Aristotle fails to provide a concrete, convincing, and comprehensive resolution. And what he does do, precisely by failing in this way, is establish in considerable detail the agenda for virtually all subsequent thinking about judgment in politics.

2
The Kantian Problematic

As we have seen, Plato and Aristotle present essentially opposite views of political judgment, Plato defining it as a kind of scientific endeavor, Aristotle specifically and pointedly denying that it is a science, although insisting that it is nonetheless a rational, truth-oriented mode of thinking, which he calls *phronēsis*. They do agree that judgment is not a mere knack, not a matter of shrewd guessing, not an irrational, mystical thing. Rather, it is, for both of them, a serious and systematic enterprise involving evidence, argument, and some type of reasoned demonstration. But they also agree about something else, something very important. Specifically, neither Plato nor Aristotle regards political judgment as a special and distinctive type of intellectual activity. It is not *sui generis*; there is no such thing as a uniquely political way of thinking. For Plato, political judgment is pretty much like any other scientific mode of thought, distinctive only because of its particular subject-matter.[1] The scientific mind is a single thing, and it proceeds more or less in the same way whether the topic is mathematics or biology or astronomy or the world of political affairs. And so too for Aristotle: practical wisdom is hardly limited to the political sphere. The virtue of *phronēsis* is suitable or required for addressing all kinds of practical problems pertaining to, for example, household management, taking care of one's body, choosing the best course of action at work, and so on.[2] Aristotle does describe in some detail the various specific kinds of political problems with which practical wisdom might be concerned. In particular, he distinguishes legislation, which is devoted to the selection of general policies for governing society, from a narrower kind of decision-making involving the application of such policies to particular cases.[3] But again, the intellectual abilities and habits that allow one to do these things well are not very different from the intellectual abilities and habits that allow one to deal effectively with a wide range of practical issues. Politics is distinctive as a particular *domain* of practical activity, but it involves and requires no special and unique *manner of thinking*.

1

In the canonical history of Western political thought, this actually turns out to be a very controversial, perhaps even unpopular, position. Indeed, the idea that politics is in fact a special kind of human endeavor, unlike any other, and that it requires a way of being in the world that is truly different and distinctive has long been a prominent and highly influential view. To be more precise, many theorists of the past have thought that politics in general and political judgment in particular require a *special kind of person*. They have argued, in effect, that the true political leader – the genuine statesman[4] – is quite unlike anybody else.

Such an approach was hardly unknown among the ancient Greeks. Indeed, the great historian Thucydides, writing about the Athenian statesman Themistocles, provides a virtually paradigmatic case in point:

> By his native genius, without preparation or supplementing it by study, he was with the briefest deliberation the most effective in decisions about immediate situations and the best at conjecturing what would happen farthest into the future; whatever he was engaged in he was capable of understanding; over matters in which he had no experience he was not incapacitated from judging adequately, and in particular he foresaw what better or worse possibilities were still concealed in the future. To sum up, this man by natural ability, with

rapid deliberation, was certainly supreme in his immediate grasp of what was necessary.[5]

Sentiments of this sort are not hard to find in Greek literature. Nonetheless, it is ancient Rome, rather than Greece, that actually provides perhaps the most systematic and influential sources of the idea of political judgment as a kind of irreducible personal quality. Writing toward the very end of the Roman republican period, for example, Cicero extols the virtues of a political aristocracy:

> [W]hen excellence governs the commonwealth, what can be more glorious? For then he who rules over others is not himself the slave of any base desire; the requirements which he lays upon his fellow-citizens he has fulfilled himself; he does not impose upon the people laws which he does not himself obey; he holds up his own life before his fellow-citizens as the law by which they may guide their lives.[6]

After nearly a century of civil war involving deep and often violent conflict between an aristocratic or senatorial elite on the one hand and champions of ordinary folk on the other, Cicero, himself one of the most famous and accomplished of Roman senators, tells us that "as long as an aristocracy guards the state, the people are necessarily in the happiest condition, since they are free from all care and anxiety." The focus here is on the *character* of those who lead. Good government means giving political authority to individuals whose personal traits of probity, intellect, experience, honor, and background make them best suited for positions of authority; and such people, in turn, are not necessarily well suited to anything other than politics. In Cicero's view, great Roman senators might not be especially adept at managing personal finances or leading armies or raising families, but their minds and their dispositions will allow them, far more than other people, both to see and to achieve the common good. True political leaders – people of sound political judgment – are, so to speak, a special category unto themselves, uniquely born and/or bred for the world of public affairs.

Cicero's discussion is typical of republican political thought; and during the subsequent period of imperial Rome – after, that is, the demise of the Republic – political writers continued to celebrate the distinctive abilities of an aristocratic elite, only this time functioning as a more or less veiled criticism of a newly dominant and anti-aristocratic autocracy. The great historian Tacitus, for example, wrote a well-known encomium in behalf of his own father-in-law Agricola, an important political and military leader who represented, in effect, the older republican or senatorial ideal as it struggled to maintain its relevance in the face of overwhelming imperial power. Tacitus says that Agricola had a "lofty, aspiring nature," but also a "sense of proportion," that "he never sought a duty for self-advancement" and "acted always with energy and a sense of responsibility," and that "to mention incorruptibility and strict honesty in a man of his caliber would be to insult his virtues" – all of which helped make him, allegedly, a paragon of practical wisdom.[7] Such a characterization was in striking contrast to what Tacitus would elsewhere describe as the decadence, corruption, and obscene immorality of despotic rulers such as Tiberius and Nero. In the various writings of Cicero, Tacitus, and many other Roman authors spanning roughly two centuries, political judgment came to be identified not primarily as an intellectual trait – not as a mode or manner of thinking – but as a function of individual character reflecting, perhaps above all, a quality of what came to be called *civic virtue* involving, at once, a strong personal commitment to serving the public good and an equally strong determination to conduct oneself with irreproachable honor.

This general way of thinking about the problem of judgment has been enormously influential. Indeed, in one form or another it has long been adopted – and adapted – by apologists for autocratic rule. We should note, of course, that in the nearly one thousand years following the decline and fall of the (Western) Roman Empire, political theorists and political practitioners could seriously contemplate no form of government other than autocracy in general and monarchy or kingship in particular. And to the degree that notions of political judgment were engaged throughout this vast period, whether explicitly or otherwise, they tended to emphasize not any particular mode or method of thinking, not a special kind of intellectual virtue or activity but, rather, the personal qualities of the monarch. In most such cases, moreover, those qualities were largely understood in terms of the ruler's allegedly close connection with God. Kings were presumed to be persons of good judgment primarily because their views were divinely inspired. Such a presumption reflected an age-old tradition, something that could be found virtually throughout recorded human history. *The Code of Hammurabi*, for example, which predates the birth of Jesus Christ by at least two thousand years, explicitly invokes God as the ultimate source of the king's law; among the Israelites of antiquity, the commandments of Moses are said to have been given directly by divine decree; the Persian king Darius, operating around the year 500 BCE, invokes the Zoroastrian god Ahura Mazda as the basis of his rule. One could offer countless other examples; and in all such cases, the monarch is, in effect, understood to be an agent of the deity, the vehicle through which God rules the world. The ultimate manifestation of this view was the development and elaboration, especially in sixteenth century Europe, of a set of theories that explicitly proposed the *divine right of kings*. According to such theories, the political judgment of the monarch is not merely good but very nearly infallible and certainly indisputable insofar as it reflects and embodies nothing less than the will of God. If the Christian God in particular is truly omniscient and benevolent, then his appointed and anointed servant – the king who, of course, wouldn't have attained the throne in the first place if God hadn't wanted him to – must be a profoundly reliable source of political wisdom. Here, again, it is the personal character of the political leader that makes for good political judgment. Specific questions about how the leader actually thinks about things – questions about the nature and process of political reasoning itself – are largely ignored.[8]

Even with the re-emergence of republican political theory during the Renaissance, writers on politics continued to focus on the personal traits of the authentic statesman. Authors such as Guicciardini and his much more famous friend Machiavelli, writing in the early sixteenth century and dealing largely with the politics of Italian city-states, produced manuals for political leaders – sometimes called "mirrors for princes" – whose goal was to describe the attitudes, habits and dispositions that would likely result in prudent or practically wise decision-making.[9] Once more, the emphasis of such materials is less on the process of judgment, understood as a manner of thinking, than on the kinds of persons who are likely to judge well, with perhaps particular attention paid to the value of experience. Indeed, one might suggest that this literature in effect adopts pretty much what both Plato and Aristotle had strenuously rejected, namely, the notion that political judgment is a kind of ineffable, almost indescribable knack, a variety of know-how or intuition that is unique to politics and that defies any kind of systematic theoretical analysis.

But whether the character of the politically wise person was thought to be aristocratic, divinely inspired, experienced, or simply clever, these various literatures naturally gave rise to certain counter-tendencies. Among other things, it would have been obvious to virtually everyone that not all well-bred Roman aristocrats were truly honorable and virtuous, not all European monarchs were persons of ability and prudence, not all individuals with know-how use their talent to positive effect; and many authors concluded from this that a focus on political judgment was itself seriously wrong-headed, perhaps even dangerous. Not only is it difficult or impossible to define either the intellectual methods or personality traits that would produce good judgment, it would be arguably even more difficult to identify and then empower those individuals who actually have the relevant qualifications. It was largely with such difficulties in mind that certain important and influential theorists of politics chose to focus on political *institutions* rather than individuals, hence on legal systems or constitutions as opposed to judgment. Consider, for example, the great Greco-Roman historian Polybius, writing in the second century BCE, who explained the astonishing achievements of the Roman republic – several centuries of comparative political stability and prosperity while also conquering enormous parts of the Mediterranean world – in largely institutional terms: "the chief cause of either success or the opposite [in politics] is, I would claim, the nature of a state's system of government."[10] According to Polybius, it is never sufficient to rely on the good judgment of political leaders. A healthy state requires, above all, a government of laws, not of persons. It is the formal structure

– the constitutional distribution of power and privilege – that counts the most. Of course, nearly two thousand years later, a quite similar view was embraced by the American founders who thought that establishing and maintaining good government was primarily a matter of constructing a sound constitution that would effectively obviate the need for political judgment. In Madison's famous phrase, "[i]f men were angels, no government would be necessary,"[11] and he insisted that the purpose of the United States Constitution was not simply to protect citizens – non-angels – from one another but also to protect them from their own leaders. Relying on the character and judgment of a political elite would be too risky, too unreliable.

If, however, political thought has historically been divided between theorists of political or civic virtue on the one hand and theorists of institutional or constitutional structure on the other, even the latter thinkers have found it difficult utterly to deny the importance of judgment. Constitutions, in and of themselves, can do only so much; institutional forms have their limits. The legal structures that constitutional systems impose are never hermetic, comprehensive, all-encompassing; there is always the need for interpretation, for filling in gaps, for applying general principles to particular cases. And thus, for every Madison who emphasized formal structures, there was a John Adams urging the importance of finding and relying on a natural aristocracy. Even Thomas Hobbes, perhaps the most rigorously systematic and formalistic of all modern theorists of politics, recognizes the important of practical wisdom. *Leviathan*, the great masterpiece of Hobbesian thought, is primarily designed logically to prove that the state, properly understood, must be governed by a unified sovereign – whether a democratic assembly, an oligarchic council or a monarch – wielding absolute and unchallenged authority over all subjects. Here we clearly have a claim about the formal, institutional structure of political society. But Hobbes also recognizes the difference between "knowledge" on the one hand and "good judgment" and "prudence" on the other. The former is largely a matter of science, the latter a matter of discernment (much like Aristotle's notion of *nous*) and experience (and as such resonates with the notion of *empeiria* against which, as we have seen, Plato argues);[12] and Hobbes clearly wants to say that judgment and prudence can in fact be crucial in helping the sovereign provide the kind of peace and prosperity for which citizens contracted in the first place and that conduces to the stability and security of the sovereign entity itself.[13]

One might say that constitutional or legal structures, however detailed and complete, are not, and cannot be, self-actuating. Their rules and principles must be implemented – given actual force – by real human beings making real decisions that affect the lives of real people in all kinds of ways. Politics is never automatic. It is always, in the end, a matter of agents individually or collectively making choices, often very difficult ones, and this tells us that the question of political judgment – what does it mean to choose well in politics and who is best suited to the task – is and will always be a fundamental problem both for political theory and for the life of any actual political society.

2

While these various theoretical positions continue to exercise considerable influence in political philosophy, contemporary debates regarding judgment have been shaped, above all, by something very different. We may call it the Kantian problematic, reflecting, as it does, the massive influence of the eighteenth-century German philosopher Immanuel Kant. This is, in a sense, peculiar. Although Kant did offer some thoughts about politics, these play a comparatively small role in his overall philosophy. His political views, moreover, embrace a fairly standard form of modern liberalism and, most important for our purposes, have little to say about political judgment itself. What Kant does provide elsewhere, however, is a powerful and enormously influential theory of judgment *per se*, and this theory now serves as the principal starting point for virtually all current thinking about practical wisdom, political or otherwise.

Kant was almost certainly the most important philosopher since Descartes and, arguably, since Aristotle. Judgment is at the absolute core of his philosophy, but it manifests itself in several ways.[14] He begins by providing a generic definition: the activity of judgment is the activity of predicating universals of particulars. This means, specifically, that to judge is to say of a particular item in the world that it is an example of or otherwise embodies some larger conceptual category or quality. We might say that the little furry, four-legged creature wagging its tail over there is a dog, and when we do so we're applying to that creature, or subsuming it under, the category or concept of dog – the quality of dog-ness. Similarly, we might say that the fire engine parked in front of my house is red, thereby predicating the category or quality of red-ness to the particular vehicle in question; or again, we might claim that the recently enacted piece of legislation is a just piece of legislation, hence that it is an example of justice. We call the category or quality a "universal," since it denotes or expresses a concept that can, in principle, be applied to an infinite number of individual things; each particular fire engine, just like each particular tomato or each particular stoplight or each particular copy of Mao Zedong's book, could be red, and there's no logical limit to how many red things there might be. The particular, on the other hand, is simply and solely the single item existing in space and time, for example, *that* little furry, four-legged creature wagging its tail over there or *that* big machine with the hook and ladder parked in front of my house or *that* particular act of Congress that the President signed into law.

Schematically, a judgment is an assertion of the form x is F, where x denotes a particular item or entity, F (or some other symbol) denotes the concept of a specific category or quality, and "is" serves as a linguistic device that performs a variety of predicative functions, depending on the judgment being expressed. Now Kant wants to say that this general formula can be and is used in some very different ways in order to express, thereby, some very different kinds of judgment. Consider the following examples:

1 That thing (x) is a tree (let's call this concept T) – which is to say that it is an example of the category or concept of tree or that it embodies the quality of tree-ness.
2 That thing (x) is an item that should not be chopped down (NC) – which is to say that it is an example of the kind

of thing, that is, the category or concept of things, that should not be chopped down.

3   That thing (*x*) is pleasantly aromatic (*PA*) – which is to say that it is an example of the type of thing that smells good.

4   That thing (*x*) is beautiful (*B*) – which is to say that it embodies the quality of beauty.

In many ways, Kant's philosophy is designed to describe exactly how these various types of claims differ from one another. As such, his project is essentially aimed at getting clear about our own linguistic usage – about the meaning of the things we say – and, thereby, to understand our own conceptual apparatus. When we say that something is a tree, exactly how is that different from saying that it shouldn't be chopped down, that it smells good and that it is beautiful? Our intuition is that these claims are not simply saying different things about the tree in question but that they are saying different *kinds* of things and that the intellectual or argumentative status of each is quite distinct from the others. Kant very much shares this intuition. He devotes his philosophy in large part to exploring and explicating the underlying and various *logics* of the several kinds of judgments that we actually do make in ordinary discourse.

When I say that the particular thing in question is a tree – as in (1) above – I am, according to Kant, doing science, roughly equivalent to what Plato calls *technē* or what Aristotle calls *theōria*. I am describing how some feature of the world actually is, hence am offering a claim about reality. This particular thing – the *x* – is an example of tree-ness (the quality of being *T*). I don't seem to be stating here a mere opinion or expressing a feeling. I purport to be describing a factual truth and to be justified in doing so. Of course, this is a very elementary form of science, but it is science nonetheless. For in saying that the thing is a tree, I am saying that it is similar to many other things that are examples of tree-ness; and I am also saying that it is not a dog, not a fire engine, not a legal statute, since it lacks the quality of dog-ness, etc. I am thereby invoking a system of categories or concepts in order to say what the thing is and what it isn't; but more than this, I am also purporting to have good reasons for classifying the object within that system. In Kant's terminology, the claim is an example of *determinate judgment*, and he means something very specific here. In determinate judgment, we bring together two elements: first, an account or description of at least some of the elements that compose the definition of the relevant concept or category; and second, an account or description of at least some of the features of the particular thing in question. In the instant case, the concept of tree (*T*) comprises a variety of more or less specific characteristics or descriptors that make the concept what it is, for example, tallness, grounded-ness, woodiness, having brown bark, having green leaves, and the like; and the particular item in front of us (*x*) is, we observe, tall, is growing in the ground, has a wooden trunk, brown bark, green leaves, and so on. In effect, the content of the concept – that which defines the very idea of tree-ness – presents a set of criteria or rules for *determining* of any particular thing whether it is or isn't a tree. We can, so to speak, test the particular thing against criteria inherent in the concept/category. In determinate judgment, our job is to determine to what extent the features of the particular thing we're judging somehow map onto the elements embedded in the concept. If the concept of tree includes the notion of having green leaves and if the particular object in front of us has green leaves, then this is at least some evidence that the object in front of us is a tree; and the more evidence of this kind that we have, the more confident we'll be that it really is a tree.

Stated otherwise, by comparing the elements that constitute the very meaning or definition of the concept with the various features of the particular thing in the world that we're thinking about, we are able to prove or justify our claim or judgment that the thing is (or, perhaps, isn't) an example – a case, an embodiment, an instantiation – of that concept. Knowing what it means for something to be a tree and knowing what the particular thing before us is like allows us to adduce evidence that will prove whether or not the thing is a tree. The evidence *determines* the outcome, hence we have made a determinate judgment.

None of this means that our judgment is necessarily correct. We can make mistakes. We can fail properly to understand the concept or quality of tree-ness and we can also fail accurately to perceive the particular object that we're looking at. To pick a different example, we might think that the whale out there is a fish because we don't really understand what makes a fish a fish; or, alternatively, we might think that the whale out there is a fish because we think, mistakenly, that it is a shark. In either case, our determinate judgment will be in error. But it is an important feature of all determinate judgments that they are, in principle, corrigible. There is a fact of the matter about what makes a fish a fish or a tree and tree, and a fact of the matter about whether the object in front of us is a whale or a shark, a tree or a bush; and this means that we can, in principle, continue to test our determinate judgments by adducing ever more evidence about the meaning of our concepts or about the accuracy of our perceptions.

According to Kant, the logic of determinate judgment is essentially two-fold. First, such judgments are *objective*. This is to say that they claim to be saying something about the thing out there – the *object* of our attention – rather than about the effect that the thing has on us, the perceiving and judging subjects. The tree is an example of the concept of tree-ness whether or not I know this and whether or not I see it that way; and when I claim that it is a tree, I am talking about a fact of the matter that is independent of my own subjective response to it. For Kant, all scientific claims purport to be objective in this way. But second, such claims also present themselves as *universal*. This is to say that when I predicate tree-ness of the object, I am in effect claiming – whether explicitly or otherwise – that everyone who is seeing and thinking clearly will necessarily agree with me. Of course, not everyone actually will agree with me all the time. You might think the tree is a bush because you don't fully understand the concept of tree; or you may think the tree is really a bush because you perceive it incorrectly. In either case, you're wrong; but from the perspective of my judgment, you're wrong because you're not seeing or thinking clearly. Of course, you might stick to your guns and claim that I'm the one who is wrong. But a defining feature of determinate judgment in particular and science in general is that such disagreements are, again at least in principle, adjudicable. We can adduce evidence regarding either the meaning of the concept or the features of the thing we're looking at. This evidence will *determine* who is right and wrong, such that everyone who recognizes the evidence will agree with the conclusion. The conclusion purports to be universally valid.

How about judgment (2) above, namely, the judgment that tree (*x*) should not be chopped down (*NC*)? This is not a scientific claim. Rather, it is, Kant would say, a moral claim, a claim about not what something is but, rather, how to treat that thing, hence a claim about what we should and should not do. To be sure, it may be the case that not all "should" claims would qualify as moral claims, but certainly many would; and so let us stipulate, in the present case, that I'm someone who believes that trees have moral rights, just like humans, and that my claim, therefore, is that it would be immoral to chop down the tree.

This is neither the time nor the place to dig very deeply into Kantian ethics – a huge and enormously complex subject. For our purposes, it will be enough to say that, for Kant, ethical claims are like scientific ones in that they purport to be both *objective* and *universal*. Here, however, the objectivity is not a matter of characterizing some features of a physical object out there in the world (as opposed to the object's effect on the perceiving subject). Rather, it is a matter of character-izing the rationality – the coherence, consistency, logical soundness – of a hypothetical moral law that I have, in effect, proposed or recommended. By saying that it would be immoral to chop down the tree, I am invoking or positing, at least implicitly, a rule or principle that is independent of my subjective choices, wishes, predilections. It stands outside of me – a thought-object, external to my personal preferences, that I purport to have discovered through sound reasoning. Again, this doesn't mean that my claim is necessarily correct. In ethics, as in science, we can make mistakes. I may have made one or more errors of reasoning; my moral claim is therefore eligible for criticism and possible revision or even refutation. This, however, doesn't change the fact that, in making a moral claim, I am purporting to be offering an objective judgment, a judgment about the moral law. Implicit in such a claim, moreover, is the further claim that anyone who reasons soundly will discover precisely the same moral law. The logic of the claim is thus not only that it is objective – pertaining, again, to the external thought-object – but that it is universally valid. One might say that Kantian moral laws are roughly analogous to mathematical theorems – thought-objects the features of which are said to be independent of any particular subjective thinker and the truth of which can be known through an assiduous application of the rules of logical inference.

For all these reasons, Kant understands particular moral judgments to be examples of *determinate judgment*, as described above. They are different in all kinds of ways from scientific judgments but are similar insofar as the features of the moral law are thought to determine the question of the morality of a particular action, for example, chopping down the tree. The action itself is the particular thing (x), which has certain distinguishing features, and the moral law is the concept or category (NC), which is composed of specific criteria for determining whether or not an action qualifies as moral.

In Kant's view, proposition (3) – the claim that the tree (x) is pleasantly aromatic or smells good (PA) – reflects a completely different logic. Two crucial elements are at play here. First, proposition (3), despite appearances, is not strictly speaking a proposition about the tree itself. Rather, it is a proposition about how the tree affects me or, even more accurately, how I react to the tree. A good smell is a form of pleasure, and so it is *my* particular state – my feeling of pleasure, of olfactory satisfaction – that is in question. Of course, I, as the observer (in this case, the thing doing the smelling), am the perceiving *subject* rather than the object perceived; and this means that the proposition is and can only be a *subjective* claim, a claim about the subject, about me.

But second, Kant's further intuition – which he shares, of course, with Plato – is that any feeling of pleasure or any similar sensual experience that manifests itself in terms of feelings or emotions is necessarily a private business. This has itself two aspects. On the one hand, I cannot know exactly how the tree smells to you. You can say that it smells good or that you find it pleasantly aromatic, just as I have, but how could we truly know that our experiences are in fact identical? The tree might smell one way to you and a very different way to me, even though both of us enjoy the experience. Feelings of pleasure or pain are inherently personal. On the other hand, and relatedly, it seems that there is no accounting for taste. For example, I might find that the tree smells good and you might find that it smells awful, which is to say that I find the smell pleasurable while you find it painful or disgusting. Who is to say which of us is correct? Indeed, the question itself seems absurd. The very idea of correct and incorrect just doesn't apply, and this suggests that there is no rule or test or criterion that would determine whether or not the tree smells good.

Consider a different case. Imagine that I'm having dinner with my four-year-old child and that I tell her to eat her spinach. She objects and tells me that she hates spinach because it tastes awful. I respond by saying no, spinach is actually quite delicious, but she makes a face and sticks to her guns. The Kantian would argue that in such a circumstance there really is, for me and my daughter, nothing more to be said. What argument could I make – what evidence could I present – to convince her that spinach is delicious; and by the exact same token, how could she convince me that it tastes bad? Of course, I could point out that millions of people love spinach, but this wouldn't affect the shudder of disgust that my daughter feels when spinach enters her mouth. She just hates the flavor; that's a fact, and that's the end of it. It is important to note that the case would be completely different if I had told her to eat her spinach not because it is delicious but because it is nutritious. She might respond to this by denying that spinach is nutritious, but here there is a great deal more that could be said. I could marshal evidence – all kinds of scientific evidence – to prove the nutritional value of spinach, and that evidence could be weighed and evaluated in order to determine to what degree we should accept its validity. I could make, in short, an objective claim about, say, the chemical or molecular properties of spinach, about the chemical or molecular properties of the human body, and about the chemical or molecular properties of the interaction among those things. Propositions about nutrition are, or purport to be, based on objective evidence; they are examples of determinate judgment. Delicious, on the other hand, is not like that at all, and neither is pleasantly aromatic or smells good. Kant wants to say that such notions, for example, notions of feeling or emotion, are indeed concepts, but that they do not have specific, identifiable elements – rules or criteria – for determining their correct application to particular things in the world. They are, in Kantian terminology, *indeterminate concepts*; their application is a matter of purely personal preference or experience, and one consequence of this is that propositions that use such concepts – propositions that predicate indeterminate concepts of particular things – are not only subjective, rather than objective, but also particular, rather than universal. Whereas the proposition that the thing is a tree embodies a logic of objectivity and universality, and whereas the proposition that the thing shouldn't be chopped down also embodies (albeit for different reasons) a logic of objectivity and universality, the proposition that the thing smells good embodies a logic of *subjective particularity*. When I claim that the tree smells good, I'm simply indicating how it smells to me and I am not at all insisting that you too should find it pleasantly aromatic. If it smells bad to you, so be it.

3

With respect to the problem of political judgment, it is proposition (4) – "That thing (x) is beautiful (B), which is to say that it embodies the quality of beauty" – that turns out to be most directly germane. In Kant's terms, (4) presents an "aesthetic" judgment, and his view is that the logic of any such judgment is quite unlike those of the other types of judgment. Specifically, to say that something is beautiful – that it has aesthetic merit – is very different from saying that it has a pleasant smell or a delicious flavor, for aesthetic claims are inherently claims of universality. If we're in a museum and I say to you that the Rembrandt is a beautiful painting, I am purporting to be making a statement not about how I feel, not about how the painting affects my emotions, not about its particular impact on my sensory apparatus but, rather, about how I react to the painting as a matter of what might be called intellectual or contemplative attitude. The painting may inspire in me any number of passions, but it may also give rise to certain dispositions of thought. It is these latter, and only them, that constitute in Kant's view an aesthetic experience. When I claim that the painting is beautiful I am essentially expressing an intellectual sensibility of some kind. In Kant's terminology, if something tastes good to me, then it "gratifies" me (the German verb is *vergnügen*) and it is "pleasurable" (*angenehm*); but if it is "beautiful" (*schön*), then it merely "pleases" me (*gefallen*) in the sense that I am favorable toward it. Insofar as I say that something is beautiful, moreover, my assertion implies that you ought to agree with me and that if you don't you're making some kind of error. As we have seen, if you fail to find the spinach delicious, that just indicates that we have different preferences or tastes; and we generally believe that there's no accounting for taste. But if you fail to see that the Rembrandt is a beautiful painting, if you fail to have the same contemplative disposition toward it that I have, then my aesthetic judgment – my assertion that the Rembrandt is beautiful – implies that your view is faulty, indeed incorrect. Inherent in my statement about the beauty of the Rembrandt is a claim about correctness that is entirely absent from my statement about, for example, the tastiness of spinach.

To say that the Rembrandt is beautiful doesn't necessarily mean that I like it – at least not in the sense that it gives me pleasure. I might find it to be – in virtue of its subject-matter or color palette or painterly style or whatever – unpleasant or depressing or disturbing or unattractive. As the cliché goes, I might not want to hang it on my wall. But I can nonetheless believe that it is a great work of art and that, as such, it embodies the fundamental aesthetic character of being beautiful; and when I claim to have indeed recognized it as such, I am simply communicating the fact that my experience with it has given rise to a certain kind of intellectual intuition that Kant associates with a judgment of beauty and that, in my view, you ought to share.

However, and at least equally important, Kant also wants to say that there is no evidence, no argument, no structure of proof that I could possibly mobilize in order to justify or defend my claim. I cannot – and will never be able to – objectively demonstrate to you or anyone else the beauty of the Rembrandt, or prove convincingly that it is more beautiful than, say, an original painting by Steinberger. If I say that you are making an error in denying that the Rembrandt is beautiful, I really have no sound basis for saying so. In this sense, though only in this sense, aesthetic judgments are just like judgments of taste, that is, judgments about whether the tree smells good or whether the spinach is delicious. Aesthetic judgments, despite demanding agreement from all other people, are deeply subjective. They describe dispositions of thought that exist *in me* and that have arisen in virtue of *my* experience of that object. They can never benefit from any kind of independent justification, even as they present themselves as valid for everyone. If both scientific and moral claims are examples of objective universal judgment, and if claims of taste are examples of subjective particular judgment, aesthetic claims are examples of *subjective universal* judgment.

Underlying this argument is the view that the relevant aesthetic concept – beauty – is an *indeterminate* concept. Unlike the concept of a tree – or of a bush or dog or fish or whale, and the like – the concept of beauty does not embrace some set of determinate features that can be used rigorously and systematically to assess particular items in the world. There is, in other words, no rule about what kind of object might or might not inspire in me the disposition of thought according to which the thing is beautiful. Again, beauty is, in this sense, rather like delicious; the idea itself offers no rules according to which it might be applied. But again, the difference is that when I wield the (indeterminate) concept of beauty – unlike the (equally indeterminate) concept of delicious – I am nonetheless insisting that everyone ought to agree with me, though for reasons that I cannot specify.

We should note further that, though deeply indeterminate, the Kantian notion of beauty – or, rather, our experience of it – is not entirely without substance. Specifically, Kant says that to have an aesthetic experience of some object is to have the contemplative intuition that it is an embodiment of what he calls "purposiveness without purpose." This is a complex technical phrase, but its basic import is actually relatively clear. Imagine that I'm hiking through the woods and happen upon a flower. Imagine, further, that while looking at the flower I suddenly have the thought that the flower is an amazing thing, that it has a certain structure, a certain kind of formal integrity and that, as such, it seems as though it were the result not of some purely natural accident, not mere chance, but, rather, of some kind of purposive entity – a creator of some type. The flower seems to be, that is, the product of an intelligent agent. I have no idea what the agent's *particular* purpose might have been; indeed, I have no reason to believe that there ever was such an agent. But my sense nonetheless is that the object is an embodiment of *some kind of* purposive impulse. Hence, purposiveness without purpose.

Such an intuition is apt to be fleeting, and quickly dismissed. After all, as a matter of determinate scientific judgment, I *know* very well that the flower is nothing other than a result of purely physical, natural processes. Science explains how the flower came about, and such an explanation has no role for an intelligent creator. But my momentary intellectual *intuition* or sense of purposiveness – my disposition of thought – was nonetheless felicitous, and in all kinds of ways. For one, it prompted me to think about how the various parts of the flower seemed to fit together in ways that made the whole thing coherent and orderly. For another, the flower seemed, during my brief epiphany, to be familiar and kindred, since I myself, just like the hypothetical and presumably fictional creator of the flower, am an intelligent agent. I am a purposive being and insofar as the flower seems to embody a kind of purposiveness, it is just like me or, rather, like something I might make. In this sense, and even if for only a moment, the natural object out there doesn't feel so alien. Walking through the forest primeval and chancing upon the flower, I suddenly – if only momentarily – feel at home; and when I reflect on all this, the result is what Kant calls "intellectual delight." It is not a feeling of physical pleasure, not like the pleasure I have when I smell the tree or eat the spinach; it is not sensuous, not an emotion. It is, instead, like the sense of satisfaction that I might have when I contemplate the wonderfully complementary curves produced by trigonometric functions. I know that these curves represent the soulless logic of mathematical thought and analysis. And yet, there are moments when they seem to suggest to me that the world is somehow suffused with intelligence and that I, as a creature of intelligence, can find in that world an accommodating home, a thought that fills

me, however briefly, with delight. When I experience intellectual delight of this kind, I am convinced of three things:
(1) the item that has inspired it is beautiful, (2) its beauty is
a fact that you should – must – recognize yourself but, (3)
if you fail to so recognize it, there's nothing I could possibly
say, no element of proof that I could marshal, to convince
you otherwise. The logic of the judgment is that it is both
universal and subjective.

4

Of course, when I see the Rembrandt painting in the museum
I know quite well that, unlike the flower, it was indeed
produced by an intelligent, purposive agent. Even here,
though, the particular dimensions of purposiveness – the
ways in which the various elements reflect some kind of
purpose – may not be immediately obvious. Nor can I ever
be sure exactly what the specific purposes might have been;
this is something of which even the artist might not be fully
aware. Thus, the feeling of surprise and intellectual delight
that I have when I intuit purposiveness without purpose in
the flower has its counterpart when I intuit in the painting a
kind of structural coherence that generally transcends – or
perhaps hides behind – the painting's apparent subject matter.
I can see that the painting is a depiction of some scene, and
I can feel as well that it arouses in me certain sentiments of,
say, sympathy or desire or sadness and the like. But I might
also, at certain brief moments, intuit some of the ways in
which its various elements come together to form an ordered
whole, and such moments of intuition constitute an aesthetic
experience of intellectual delight. Kant believes that it is
there, and only there, that one truly finds the beauty of the
painting.

   With respect to art, then, Kant is a severe formalist.
Intellectual delight – the sense of beauty – is a matter of
intuiting in the object a kind of orderly, well-structured,
intelligently crafted composition, a pleasing (though not
necessarily pleasurable) arrangement of elements. We often
say that the brilliantly yellow color of light in the painting – or,

similarly, the sumptuous sound of the violin in the concerto – is beautiful. But according to Kant, when we say that, we misspeak. The yellow of the paint, or the tone of the violin, moves us, makes us feel pleasure, stirs our passion, brings tears to our eyes. But those are purely sensual reactions, like the taste of spinach. They are subjective, and also particular. They imply nothing about universal validity. Very different from this is the contemplative delight that accompanies an intuition of the painting's formal integrity or of the concerto's compositional integrity. Here is a kind of thoughtful satisfaction that, though certainly subjective, seems nonetheless as if it should transcend our own particularity.

For Kant, aesthetic judgments are examples of what he calls "reflective judgment" and are, as such, to be sharply distinguished from all kinds of determinate judgment. In determinate judgment – whether scientific or ethical in nature – we have access to a concept or universal prior to our engagement with the particular thing. This access involves enumerating those factors that the concept embraces; and with such an enumeration in mind, we can compare the elements of the concept to the features of the particular thing that we happen to be observing and, on that basis, decide whether or not the thing is an example of the concept. The process is, so to speak, top down. The elements of the universal – the aspects that define the concept – are used to determine whether the actual object in the world does or does not fit the definition. In reflective judgment, on the other hand, the process is (roughly) reversed. We observe items in the world (e.g., the flower, the painting, etc.), and, if and when they give rise to intuitions of purposiveness without purpose, we say that they are beautiful. The concept of beauty itself is thus defined as nothing other than the set of beautiful things. The content of the concept doesn't determine but, rather, *reflects* our engagement with those things. Its definition, if it can be called that, is without determinate content. If I ask you about the meaning of beauty, the best you can do is point to putative examples of beauty. You cannot say, in any determinative way, why those things are beautiful, since there is no specific account of beauty that could provide such an explanation. Since, moreover, the claim that some particular thing is beautiful can only be a case of *subjective* universal validity, the concept of beauty – that is, the list of examples of those things thought to be beautiful – can never give rise to *objective* truth.

Kant's analysis of reflective judgment is not limited to questions of aesthetics. In his view, it applies as well to matters of "teleological judgment" or what we can call functional causation. Causation of this kind pertains in particular to our understanding of organisms, which compose an extremely important aspect of reality as we conceive it. Indeed, the analysis of organisms is, for Kant, essential to the scientific enterprise.

An organism is generally thought of as some kind of unified structure composed of distinct parts or components – "organs" – in which the identity and good health of the whole is dependent on the identity and good health of the parts and, at the same time, the identity and good health of the parts depends on the identity and good health of the whole. The human body is an example. A human body is an organism that contains, among many other things, a liver. Containing a liver is an aspect – though obviously only one aspect – of what makes a human body a human body; and having a healthy liver is an aspect of what it means to have a healthy body. By the same token, a liver is really a liver only insofar as it exists and operates within a human body. Cut out the liver and the liver dies, as does the body. Whole depends on part, part on whole.

This dependence, moreover, is essentially thought of as a matter of function. The liver is supposed to do certain things for the body, and the body – in virtue of its other organs – is supposed to do certain things for the liver. We say, then, that what *causes* a liver to be a liver is the particular *function* that it performs in the body. This is, in effect, a theory of the liver, a theory of functional causation. The existence and nature of the liver is causally *explained* by its function in the body.

Kant wants to emphasize that the analysis of functionality is an essential part of our scientific engagement with the world – in this case, the science is biology – and yet, at the same time, sharply different from the more conventional scientific approach to causation. In much or most of science, and in much or most of ordinary life, we understand the world in general to be a system or series of causes and effects. We try to understand the world by trying to discover what causes what. Three features stand out. First, causes and effects are distinct from and independent of one another. A baseball bat is one thing, a baseball is another; each is what it is independent of the other – a baseball is a baseball even if there is no bat around; and so when the bat hits the ball and the ball sails over the fence, or dribbles toward second base, this is a matter of one thing mechanically causing some change or event in another different thing. Second, the cause–effect relationship is always directional. It goes *from* cause *to* effect. The ball's motion doesn't cause the bat's motion. Rather, it is exactly the reverse. Mechanical causation is, in this respect, asymmetrical. Third, there is a particular and necessary temporal relationship between cause and effect. The cause always precedes the effect in time. The ball doesn't sail over the fence and then the bat hits it; it has to be the other way around. All of this is crucial for Kant, because he believes that humans – all humans – are endowed with fundamental intuitions of space and time and that these uniquely allow us to make *determinate* judgments of mechanical causation. Given our intuitions, that is, given the cognitive spatial and temporal capacities of the human mind, we can prove and demonstrate that the bat caused the ball to sail over the fence. This is something that we can know with real certitude; and here is the basis for scientific knowledge in the usual sense. It is the foundation of what Kant calls *cognition*. Just as the elements of the concept of a tree and the observations of the features of that particular leafy thing over there allows us to know – to make a determinate judgment – as to whether or not the thing is a tree, so do intuitions of space and time together with our observations of the motion of the bat and the motion of the ball allow us to know whether or not the bat caused the ball to sail over the fence.

Notice, however, that the relation of body to liver is quite different. First, as we have seen, these are not two independent things. The body is what it is (partly) in virtue of the existence and activity of the liver, the liver in virtue of the role it plays in the body. Second, there is here no single directionality in the causal relationship. Body causes liver and liver causes body. They are mutually causing, and neither is primary. Finally, there is, of course, no temporal ordering either. The body didn't come first, nor did the liver. They both developed, and they both operate, simultaneously. Kant's view is that these features are crucial. They are features that cannot be accounted for by those fundamental intuitions of space and time that compose the essential elements of human cognition and knowledge, and that allow for determinate judgments. As such, they defy proof or explanation. How do you prove that the liver was created *in order to* perform certain functions that the body needs or that the body was created *in order to* develop a healthy liver? Such claims seem to presuppose, without being able to demonstrate, a kind of purposiveness similar to the purposiveness that we attribute to beautiful objects. Functional claims, like aesthetic claims, are therefore matters of reflective rather than determinate judgment, and this makes them both extremely interesting and highly problematic. In the example we have been looking at, biology and medical science cannot proceed unless it is understood that the liver's purpose is to perform certain functions for the body. If you ask a doctor about the liver, he or she will almost certainly provide a functional account. Indeed, a doctor who cannot do this isn't much of a doctor. But while we can prove that the liver actually performs certain functions, we cannot prove that this *explains* its existence. The resort to functional causality as a mode of explanation is an assumption, a presupposition, not the result of a scientific demonstration. As such, it is, like aesthetic judgment, not a matter of knowledge or truth or cognition. Reflective judgments with respect to functionalism in organisms, like reflective judgments with respect to the beauty of aesthetic objects, are *non-cognitive*.

It turns out that the implications of this for the problem of political judgment are immense. Kant's theory of judgment is, as we have seen, two-fold. On the one hand, normal science, and much of everyday life, operates on the basis of determinate judgment, hence is a matter of cognition, knowledge, and truth. To the degree that this is taken to be a model for politics, political judgment will be regarded as a kind of scientific enterprise, roughly as Plato had suggested. On the other hand, important regions of human endeavor, involving claims about beauty and functionality, are matters of reflective judgment, and do not allow for proof or demonstration.

They are non-cognitive activities and, as such, cannot make serious claims to truth. To the degree that political judgment is thought to be a species of reflective judgment, it too will be understood as a fundamentally non-cognitive type of thought or discourse having rather little to do with truth. And this, it turns out, is where a great deal of present-day thinking about political judgment has gone, specifically under the influence of Kant.

3
The Arendtian Theory
of Judgment

The importance of Kantian reflective judgment for contemporary thinking about political judgment is largely attributable to Hannah Arendt. Born and raised in Germany during the first part of the twentieth century, a refugee from European anti-Semitism who emigrated to the United States in 1940, Arendt was a political theorist of extraordinary importance whose work continues to be astonishingly influential. Its influence reflects a series of brilliant writings that develop a unique and compelling vision of the very nature of political life itself, emphasizing the absolutely central role that political judgment ought to play in the realm of public affairs and exploring in detail the question of exactly what it means to have good judgment in politics.

1

In *The Human Condition*, her masterpiece, Arendt endeavors to describe and analyze nothing less than the full range of human activity in the world.[1] She seeks, specifically, to develop a complete and exhaustive typology of the different kinds of things that we actually do. Our doings compose what she calls the *vita activa* – the active life of humans – and she argues that they fall into three broad categories: labor, work and Action. Arendt's terminology is perhaps idiosyncratic, but the conceptual distinctions she has in mind are, at least up to a point, clear enough. And again, their influence has been enormous.

All humans engage in *labor*, by which Arendt means activity that is oriented to the care and well-being of the physical body. In this respect, humans are not much different from animals; indeed, it is primarily in labor that we manifest the animal side of our nature. Like animals, we eat, we seek shelter from the elements, and we protect ourselves from dangers posed by other creatures, human and otherwise. These are for us, as they are for animals, part of who we are. It is true that humans, unlike animals, can go on diets or fasts or hunger strikes, that they can choose to expose themselves to the elements by singing in the rain, that they can court danger by jumping out of airplanes or wrestling with alligators. But in the end, even people who do such things endeavor to eat, stay warm, and find safety – if, that is, they want to exist as humans. According to Arendt, it is through labor that we achieve these ends. Labor thus describes the actual things we do – farming, wage earning – in order to feed, clothe, and house ourselves, and all such activity has certain characteristics. First, labor is driven by need. We may have an opportunity to choose what we eat and how we obtain it, but those choices will be limited and constrained by the basic requirements of the body and by the vicissitudes of nature. Labor is not notably a realm of freedom. Second, the need for food, shelter and safety and for the kind of activity that produces such things is something that we all share equally. The differences in our bodies are, in these respects, trivial compared to our common dependence on protein, water, sleep, warmth, and our common capacity for toil. In labor, we are all, in the end, pretty much alike. Finally, the process of labor by which we obtain what we need, like the process of consumption itself, typically unfolds according to regular, rhythmic, repetitive natural patterns. At certain times of the day your body demands food or rest, at certain times of the year the world allows you to plant and grow and harvest the food you need, at certain times in the life-cycle you will mature into adulthood, toil in the fields or factories, reproduce yourself, die. In short, the activity of labor, despite its untold superficial variations, is at base a matter of *necessity*, of *homogeneity* and of *predictability*. You may labor in the fields or on the seas or in the mines, I may labor in the factory or on the chain-gang or at a desk, but in all such cases laboring involves some manner of more or less routine, patterned activity designed, in one way or another, to, as we say, put food on the table, and all ultimately governed by the cyclical rhythms of nature. The ultimate indicator of the essence of physical or biological existence is, perhaps ironically, death itself. Death is inevitable, it is shared equally by all, and it is, within fairly narrow parameters, perfectly predictable.

But humans also work, and for Arendt this is very different from labor. Work is the activity of making things. Of course, one might want to say that we make things in labor as well. The farmer makes – grows – the wheat that the miller uses to make the flour that the baker uses to make the bread. But all such making is subservient to the needs of the body and the thing that is made is designed specifically to be consumed, to be destroyed – for example, ingested – almost as soon as it comes into existence. In work, on the other hand, we make things that are designed to last, things whose purpose is not to satisfy the momentary, recurrent, biological needs of the body but to introduce objects that help compose the very world in which we live.

Consider, for example, the kitchen table, understood as something that someone – a furniture maker – has crafted through work. It is true that a kitchen table is useful in helping us consume the food that we eat in order to stay alive. To that extent, it serves the labor-oriented demands of the physical body. But we certainly don't *need* the table to do that; and indeed, the table does much more. As we sit around the table and eat our dinner, it creates a kind of space that establishes relationships among us. The table separates us. You're eating your meal over there, I'm eating mine over here. But it also organizes us. You're at the head of the table, I'm sitting by your side and across from my friend. As such, it not only separates us but connects us. Sitting down "at table" means that we're eating dinner together, that we're eating, indeed, the same meal even though, in another sense, we're eating different meals. The table creates, in effect, a small society of people and creates it in a certain way; and so too for the untold other products of work – chairs, rooms, houses, offices, landscapes, works of art, basketball courts, altars, chess boards, library shelves, and so on – that establish what Arendt calls a "world" and on the basis of which we relate ourselves to one another, establishing our separations and our linkages. Unlike labor, there is no purely physical or biological necessity here. In work, we are free to create the relationships – hence the relationship-creating objects – that we want to create. Unlike labor, there is no obvious uniformity here either. Indeed, individuals and groups of individuals differentiate themselves by creating different objects that generate different kinds of relationships or social entities. And unlike labor, the process of work is typically not governed by the rhythms of physical nature. Objects of work are made by artisans – craftsmen, architects, sculptors, and painters – creative people who take pride in producing "works" of quality that are not immediately consumed but that will endure and that will help establish a more or less permanent environmental structure in which we can situate ourselves vis-à-vis one another in intelligent and intelligible ways.

It should be noted that Arendt is a sharp critic of modernity, and part of her criticism involves what she sees as the declining importance of work in favor of labor. Increasingly, human activity is devoted to the mass production of consumer objects that reflect fashion and fad, that are designed to be destroyed and replaced in systems of planned obsolescence, that embody the need of late capitalist society constantly to feed a voracious, ever growing, and increasingly hegemonic structure of relentless buying and selling. Here, the habits and dispositions of labor, hardly bad in and of themselves insofar as they serve real physical needs, are perversely transferred into the larger world of commerce. We become, as a result, ever more animalistic and mindless, even as our imaginative and technological capacity to produce sky-rockets.

If, however, modernity is guilty of devaluing or marginalizing work, it is at least equally guilty of devaluing or marginalizing Action. This is a technical term in Arendt, and

I capitalize it in order to distinguish it from the more general or generic concept of action. In Arendt's thought, Action is roughly synonymous with politics. As such, it is sharply different from the other aspects of the *vita activa*, precisely because political life itself is different. For Arendt, the world of politics is *sui generis*, a distinctive and unique way of being in the world, irreducible to labor or work or any other possible type of human endeavor. The political world is a world like no other.

In brief, the basic facts of politics are different from other kinds of facts. They are, in a word, "haphazard," and their reach and development is "boundless." According to Arendt:

> Action, though it may proceed from nowhere, so to speak, acts into a medium where every reaction becomes a chain reaction and where every process is the cause of new processes. Since action acts upon beings who are capable of their own action, reaction, apart from being a response, is always a new action that strikes out on its own and affects others. Thus, action and reaction among men never move in a closed circle and can never be reliably confined to two partners. (1959, 69)

When we engage in politics – when we propose an idea for our community, or propagate an ideology, or suggest a policy or a law or a different way of organizing ourselves or a different way of making decisions – we are necessarily venturing into unexplored terrain, and the results are literally and inherently unpredictable. True political endeavor never occurs within a manageable or reliable framework. When we engage in Action, we necessarily affect other people, who then are apt, in turn, to engage in Action that affects still other people, and so on; but because the people so affected are free and diverse, the causal chain is utterly different from the kinds of regular, repetitive, and predictable causal chains that scientists seek to study. When we Act, we can never be certain of what will happen: "… the strength of the action process is never exhausted in a single deed but, on the contrary, can grow while its consequences multiply …. The reason why we are never able to foretell with certainty the outcome and end of any action is simply that action has no end. The process of a single deed can quite literally endure throughout time until mankind itself comes to an end" (1959, 209).

For Arendt, this implies that politics, properly understood, is a realm of novelty, freedom, and plurality. *Novelty*, in this context, means that in politics we tend to propose things that are truly new, innovative, and unexpected, hence very different from the kinds of highly predictable outcomes that we find in the on-going processes of natural, physical, and biological cause and effect, and different as well from the rule-governed processes of following a pattern or blueprint in order to make something durable. *Freedom* here means that politics is not governed by the needs of the body or the demands of an ever-widening system of production and consumption, for in politics we make rules rather than follow them. *Plurality* means that we are sharply different from one another in our dispositions, orientations, and beliefs, and in ways that demand a kind of innovative, imaginative, and visionary engagement with the world and with each other. On this basis, we can create a public space that constitutes nothing less than a community – a polity – in which we will continue to deal with one another in innovative, imaginative, and visionary ways and, thereby, continually re-create that community.

Politics, so understood, is a risky business. The boundlessness and unpredictability of the public sphere requires courage and audacity. It eschews formulas. It resists the demands of nature, of economics, of psychology, of fashion and fad. It seeks after ideals, principles, and revelations even as it doggedly resists turning those ideals, principles, and revelations into ossified and confining structures of unfreedom.

For Arendt, a model case of true political Action was the activity of the American Founding Fathers in (re)creating the United States, first by declaring and establishing its independence and then by writing and re-writing its basic laws. On her account, the Founders risked life and limb in order to invent a new political science, then used their experience and imagination to formulate a new conception of a political order that would reflect the complex ideals of democratic self-government, competent and skillful administration, and a stable and orderly way of life. In doing so, they modeled one of the principle virtues of political Action as Arendt understands it, namely, the virtue of political judgment.

2

In what, then, did the political judgment of the Founders consist and, on this basis, how should we characterize political judgment in general? It is here that Arendt invokes Kant. Her interpretation of Kant is, to say the least, idiosyncratic. While Kant himself did write a bit about politics, Arendt essentially ignores that writing altogether. In her view, the Kantian notion of reflective judgment – which, as we have seen, emerges in the context of aesthetic and functionalist issues and without any serious mention of politics itself – in fact constitutes Kant's real political philosophy. As such, it forms the basis for Arendt's theory of political judgment.

Just as Arendt describes three ways of acting in the world – labor, work, and action – so does she describe three corresponding ways of thinking about the world: logical reasoning, cognition, and Thought. Again, Arendt's terminology may be eccentric. But again, her conceptual apparatus is incisive and challenging.[2]

Arendt describes *logical reasoning* as a kind of intellectual "labor power," thereby linking the intellectual process of logic with the physical processes of biologically oriented endeavor. In her view, logical reasoning is like labor in that it operates according to systems of strict necessity. A logical conclusion is not a matter of free choice. To the exact opposite, it describes an outcome that is imposed upon us by the rigid laws of thought and rational inference. Moreover, those laws are universal. What is logically true for me must be logically true for you and for everyone else. Arendt insists that the processes of logical reasoning are rooted in the physiology of the human brain. She doesn't present much evidence in support of this claim, and it is an interesting claim to consider in the light of recent developments in cognitive science, but its clear force is to connect logical reasoning with the body and to suggest that it operates in a kind of rote, automatic, almost mindless fashion that pays little attention to the nuances and complexities of human and social variety and choice.

Cognition, as Arendt uses the term, is different altogether. For her, it describes a kind of thinking that is fundamentally instrumental or goal-oriented. It always has a particular substantive intention – often or usually the intention of trying to make something – and this means that it is typically connected not with labor but with work. It is a matter of means to ends thinking, and one implication is that there are different kinds of cognition depending on the different kinds of ends that one is seeking. The cabinet maker who sets out to build a kitchen table, and who does so with a particular concept or model of the table in mind, is engaged in a different kind of thought process from the chef who wants to create a dish, or the architect who wants to build a building, or the painter who wants to paint a painting. Logical reasoning is purely formal. In cognition, on the other hand, form and content are inextricably connected with one another. How you think depends on what you want to make. Moreover, in cognition, unlike logical reasoning, there are choices. The craftsman is, at least in principle, free to decide what to make and different craftsmen will make different things or, indeed, different versions of the same thing. Not all kitchen tables are alike. Nonetheless, cognition is also a matter of following rules, of learning a skill – an "art" – that describes and prescribes the right method for doing something. There is a correct way to think like a cabinet maker, and this suggests that the freedom and diversity of cognition, as a mode of thought, is both real and severely limited.

But Arendt thinks that humans have the capacity for yet another kind of intellectual endeavor, and this she terms *Thought*. As with Action, I capitalize the term in order to distinguish Arendt's usage from ordinary usage. Arendtian Thought is radically unconstrained. It is what happens when we let our ideas take flight, when we resist and violate accepted modes and methods of analysis, when we try to break the intellectual mould, imagine new possibilities, create previously unknown ways of looking at things, explore bold and innovative pathways. The results of Thought cannot be predicted or accounted for in terms of pre-established rules or methods. They do not fit – they reject – common patterns; and, partly as a consequence of this, they come in all sorts of varieties. Thought is, in short, an embodiment of novelty, freedom, and plurality. As such, it is the natural intellectual partner of Action. If logical reasoning describes how the mind operates as a form of intellectual labor power, and if cognition describes how it functions in work, Thought describes how it manifests itself in Action, hence in politics. As such, Thought is the foundation and essence of political judgment. Political judgment is, for Arendt, the form that Thought takes in the public world, the world of human affairs, properly understood (1971, 446).

Arendt draws several implications. First, political judgment is not oriented toward, perhaps not even concerned with, truth. Logical reasoning involves truth claims understood in terms of coherence; cognition involves truth claims understood in terms of mechanical cause and effect, that is, from means to ends. As such, both are examples of Kantian determinate judgment. Political judgment, on the other hand, as a mode of Thought, is a matter of reflective judgment. And just as Kantian aesthetics and functional analysis are non-cognitive in the sense of being utterly unable to prove or definitively justify their claims, so do the fruits of Arendtian political judgment resist efforts at demonstration or justification. Political judgment is not a matter of rational argument, in the conventional sense of the term. A good political judgment is not to be understood as true.

But if the goal of political judgment is not the discovery of truth, then what is it? Arendt's answer is clear: political judgment, like Thought in general, aims at agreement. Again, this is much like Kant. In Kantian aesthetics, my claim that something is beautiful, or that it can be explained functionally, is a claim that I cannot prove but that I offer in the conviction that you should nonetheless agree with it. It is something that demands your assent, though it does so without adducing evidence. In a similar fashion, the goal of Thought, for Arendt, is not to discover a fact or prove a theorem but, rather, to attach a concept to an experience so as to render that experience meaningful and intelligible in ways that somehow seem to you convincing or appropriate and that you can therefore accept. It asks you to nod your head, to assert without being able to prove, that what has been said somehow seems right or persuasive or resonant. And insofar as political judgment is a matter of Thought, its goal is to create a web of on-going, public relationships among a plurality of individuals and to sustain, thereby, a structure of shared understandings and practices on the basis of which we can create and enjoy a community.

Arendt thus embraces a sharply non-cognitivist theory of political judgment. In this respect, she rejects both the Platonic and Aristotelian approaches. Recall that Plato thought of political judgment as a kind of rational science; and while Aristotle distanced himself from this, he nonetheless insisted that *phronēsis* or practical wisdom is indeed a certain type of truth-oriented thinking. Arendt's view is radically different. Again, political judgment aims at agreement rather than truth; and one consequence of this is to connect Action – hence politics – very closely to the art of persuasion or rhetoric. Whereas much of the Western philosophical tradition – including both Plato and Kant – had excoriated rhetoric as a tool of deceit, irrationality, superstition, and falsehood, Arendt celebrates it as a fundamental source of solidarity and community. For her, speech – the artful use of words that resonate with an audience and that shape and direct the process of public spirited deliberation – becomes the political skill par excellence. The ability effectively to communicate the fruits of Thought and political judgment is, in this respect, the very foundation of Action, of politics itself, properly so conceived. And what we have here, then, is nothing less than the aestheticization of politics in general and political judgment in particular. Far from being a routine, prosaic, algorithmic process of production and consumption as with labor or a rule-governed, goal-driven, methodical enterprise as with work, the activity of the true political leader is closer to that of a poet – an inspired, imaginative, audacious effort to construct a web of meaning, free from the grubby demands of commerce and devoted to the elucidation and inspiring elaboration of shared and deep-seated hopes and ideals.

3

If Arendt is largely responsible for the centrality of Kant for the contemporary literature on political judgment, Ronald Beiner is perhaps primarily responsible for the continuing influence of Arendt herself. His important book, *Political*

Judgment,[3] covers much the same territory as the present book, only in more depth and with greater sophistication; his edition of Arendt's *Lectures on Kant's Political Philosophy*, moreover, includes a lengthy and influential interpretive essay.[4] Together, these works arguably inaugurate the contemporary discourse on political judgment in the English-speaking world, hence help establish the generally Arendtian flavor of the contemporary discussion.

For Beiner, as for Arendt, political judgment is explicitly described as a kind of Kantian reflective judgment. In this context, he strenuously denies that judgment is a matter of following rules. There are at least two aspects to this. Either in making a judgment we do not have access to, and do not invoke or rely on, any kind of formal procedure, protocol, or algorithm – judgment involves "a human capacity for non-algorithmic action" (131) – or else, if there are rules for acting, we have no access to any kind of formal procedure, protocol, or algorithm for selecting the correct rule to follow. Specifically:

> [W]hatever rules are available must be applied to the particular situation in hand, and this application cannot itself be dictated by a rule, for then one would fall into an infinite regress of rule governing rule governing rule and so on. Human agents are not subject to such regress because rule-application for them itself presupposes knowing what it is to apply a rule, which is in turn not dictated by a rule.[5]

Beiner mentions several examples of reflective judgment – playing a game, preparing a meal, composing a letter, decorating a room, designing a work of art, engaging in acts of rhetorical persuasion – but at one point pays especially close attention to the activity of playing chess. While chess is, of course, a rule-governed endeavor, the act of actually choosing which move to make is not a matter of following a strict step-by-step decision process. Rather, it requires "the need to imagine fresh possibilities [which] introduces an element of freedom into the game, to such an extent that the full diversity of appropriate moves is unlikely to be absolutely exhausted by programmes fed into a digital computer." It is important to note here that at the time Beiner was writing, computers were unable to defeat the best human chess masters. This is no longer the case, which may suggest that chess does indeed lend itself to algorithmic endeavor; and if that is true of chess, might it be true of a great many other things as well? Of course, the success of computers in chess does not itself contradict the claim that the best human players, in making their moves, proceed not on the basis of algorithms but, rather, in terms of some kind of reflective judgment in which they "actually draw upon a 'subsidiary' awareness of [their] position that cannot be formalized, and 'zero in' on what strike [them] as promising possibilities on the basis of such tacit (and non-rule-governed) awareness." Indeed, in saying this Beiner offers, I would suggest, a paradigmatic case of Arendtian theorizing about reflective judgment (though it may be interesting to speculate as well about its connection to Aristotelian perspectives). Good chess playing, and presumably good judgment in politics and elsewhere, is perhaps more like an art than a science.

Such an account, however, raises a variety of questions. Among other things, it is not easy to know exactly how good judgment is to be executed. As indicated, Beiner says that the good chess player "draws upon subsidiary awareness," but it is not clear how this happens. It is specifically unclear how one distinguishes productive, prudent, relevant, and effective aspects of subsidiary awareness from less productive aspects. If the good chess player is to "zero in" on what strikes him or her as promising, how does he or she do that? How do we separate the promising possibilities from the less promising ones? In attempting – at least implicitly – to answer such questions, Beiner adverts to the faculty of "imagination." The good chess player, like the person of good judgment in general – including political judgment – must exercise his or her capacity to imagine things. But what capacity is that, how is it exercised, and how do we distinguish good imagination from bad? One worries, on the one hand, that a kind of mysticism is being invoked here. This seems to be not at all what Beiner intends, but the problem is to figure out how he can avoid it. Imagination might be some kind of occult faculty that operates in strange ways – ways that defy the logic of rules – and that remains undefined, unspecified, elusive, like the kind of knack that, as we have seen, Plato disparaged. On the other hand, one worries also that imagination, as it operates in Beiner's account, is effectively little more than a synonym for judgment. Those who have imagination have, perhaps by definition, good judgment, and such an account, if accurate, doesn't advance our understanding of what judgment itself actually is and how it functions. Along these lines, then, Beiner says that the person of imagination and judgment "conjures up" answers as to how to proceed – that is, the proper course of action – but says rather little about what it actually means to conjure something up and how one might know whether one is doing it well or badly. Indeed, the verb to conjure is often connected with notions of magic, and that hardly seems a promising and reliable foundation for understanding, implementing, and identifying good judgment, in politics and elsewhere.

In the face of this, Beiner nonetheless insists that "standards of rationality are operative" in judgment, that the person of good judgment adduces "various grounds" for showing that a choice was "appropriate" – where an appropriate choice is, presumably, a good choice – hence that judgment is not simply magical but, rather, rests on some kind of argumentative, reasoned foundation. It remains unclear, however, what those standards of rationality might be, since rationality is generally understood as, among other things, a matter of following and being governed by the rules or laws of thought. Beiner says that "one cannot 'prove' that one's judgment was the right one," but that "one can point to various features of the particular situation that justify one's choice." The worry here is that a straw-man is being refuted. It is not clear that the inability to develop a definitive proof is sufficient to say that something like a Platonic, scientific, rationalistic account of judgment is thereby ruled out. Science itself is almost always a matter of provisional, hence non-absolute, truth-claims replacing earlier provisional, non-absolute truth-claims as inquiry unfolds over time, and surely this involves applying the rules or algorithms of the scientific method to generate proofs. How, indeed, does one "justify" anything as being appropriate, good, effective, or right without the justification functioning as a kind of proof, however suggestive and tentative it might be. Ultimately, Beiner says that a good judgment is one that is "rationally affirmed, not 'proven,'" and it is not easy to discern in a statement such as this what could count as "rational."

4

Despite, or perhaps because of, its enormous influence, Arendt's theory of Action, Thought, and political judgment has been subjected to serious criticism. Perhaps the most widespread pertains to what some readers see as her utter lack of interest in questions of justice and in specific issues of equality, poverty, oppression, and fairness. As a result of this, her work is often seen as tangential at best, irrelevant at worst, to the real world of public affairs; and an indifference to questions of justice is sometimes taken as an acceptance of and even a passive, if unwitting, support for the forces of inequality and unfairness.

One might well say that the focus of the modern state, and the focus of much political thought since the Renaissance, has been on providing peace and prosperity for citizens and ensuring that such peace and prosperity is shared by all citizens alike according to principles of justice. As John Rawls, an important twentieth century inheritor of this tradition, says, justice is the principal virtue of the political state. In such a context, liberals, monarchists, socialists, communists, and others disagree not so much about the centrality of these kinds of concerns; rather, they disagree about what the idea of justice is and, relatedly, about why states often fail to provide the requisite peace and prosperity.

From an Arendtian perspective, all of this seems like a colossal category mistake. To focus on peace and prosperity is to focus on the needs and desires of the body. It is to understand politics as subsumed under – virtually as an agent of – economics, hence to conceive of political endeavor as fundamentally a part of labor, emphasizing its role in sustaining effective systems of production and consumption. Notions of justice, fairness, and human thriving are simply defined in terms of the distribution of goods and services; political life is about generating and allocating wealth. Such a focus, on an Arendtian view, undermines the possibilities of real Action and authentic political judgment. Politics becomes a matter of calculation, and the human capacity for courageous and audacious endeavor, for visionary and imaginative Thought, for real political judgment that establishes, through inspiring speech and bold deeds, new and meaningful conceptions of community – all of this is extirpated by the relentless and deadening demands of buying and selling.

Critics of Arendt insist that her notion of politics entirely ignores the really important issues: hunger, insecurity, injustice, oppression, violence, prejudice, fear. However prosaic and ordinary these issues might be, clearly their consequences for real people are profound in the extreme. Shouldn't they be our main concern? Isn't solving such real-world problems precisely what real-world politics – and real political judgment – is and ought to be about? By ignoring or under-emphasizing problems of this kind, doesn't Arendt's theory entirely miss the point?

The criticism may be unfair, and there is a large literature on the "social question" in Arendt. But underlying the criticism is a much deeper one. It is the non-cognitivism of Arendt's conception of political judgment – its rejection of the notion of truth and, in particular, moral truth – that raises real red flags. In this respect, Kant himself would, I think, be among Arendt's harshest critics. As we have seen, Kant's theory of reflective judgment is, indeed, a form of non-cognitivism; but as such, it is sharply distinguished from Kantian ethics, which is, as we have also seen, a matter of determinate judgment. Kant, in other words, very much believes in demonstrable moral truth – objective moral truth – and certainly under-stands such truth to be fundamental in addressing the deeply and inherently moral issues that are characteristic of public life. The Arendtian impulse to aestheticize politics and political judgment, to see it as separate not only from scien-tific truth but from ethical truth as well, and explicitly to see morality in public life as inherently weak and ineffectual – according to Arendt, and as the saying goes, "nice guys always finish last" – is disturbing indeed. How, for example, would Arendtian theory distinguish the good political leader possessed of good political judgment from the dangerous, destructive, perhaps evil leader who might be courageous, audacious, innovative, rhetorically gifted and inspiring, even as he or she leads his or her followers into hell? History seems to be replete with such individuals.

Against such a criticism, Arendt might appear to have a defense, namely, in her reliance on what she calls common sense. This is yet another notion derived from Kant, and Arendt seems to think that it does indeed provide a kind of test both for identifying good political judgment and for protecting against despotism. Good judgment is judgment that, as we say, simply makes common sense. It is something that we recognize when we see it, even if we are unable to enumerate any of its relevant determinate characteristics, of which there are none. Plain old common sense would tell us, for example, that Mussolini was dangerous, that Hitler was the very embodiment of evil, that Stalin would rival Hitler in iniquity. One wouldn't need any kind of complex theory or proof to know those things.

The trouble is that Arendt's notion of common sense is vague as best. And if we investigate the idea in some detail, it turns out to motivate a conception of political judgment that is, in fact, very different from what Arendt has proposed. Indeed, the important idea of common sense is precisely a basis for doubting, rather than embracing, the Arendtian approach to judgment.

5

It is with some such criticisms in mind that Linda Zerilli has produced both a systematic reformulation and a strenuous defense of the Arendtian approach to judgment.[6] Her work at once echoes Beiner's appropriation of Arendt's theory and seeks to revise that appropriation so as to develop a more adequate notion of judgment, understood as a principal feature of a healthy democratic politics. The degree to which Zerilli provides a satisfactory account, both of Arendt's thought in particular and of the problem of judgment in general, remains, however, an open question.

Like Beiner, Zerilli stakes out a strongly "anti-intellectu-alist" position: good political judgment is emphatically not a matter of discovering and following strict, rational rules, algorithms, or other kinds of systematic, proof-oriented processes that have as their aim the establishment of objective truth. Judgment, for Zerilli as for Beiner, is not at all scientific. But unlike Beiner, she also denies that judgment is therefore non-cognitive. In effect, she wants to have it both ways or, perhaps more accurately, wants to deny that there is or need be any strong distinction between reasoned thought on the one hand and subjective opinion on the other. Her aim is "not to exclude the relevance of cognition to politics [but] to emphasize the reflective and affective character of all judgment, aesthetic and empirical."[7] In her view, "to deny that the scientific model of rationality can be extended to all registers of human practice and judgment is not to concede an untenable relativism."[8] Her goal, then, is to show how we can have a robust notion of truth without committing ourselves to rationalistic, rule-based forms of demonstration.

Zerilli's approach involves, in part, a reinterpretation of Arendt's work itself. According to this reinterpretation, Arendt is not really as hostile to truth in politics as many readers have supposed. Rather, she is hostile to *proof* in politics. The standard intellectualistic notion that truth is a matter of proof – that truth claims should be taken as true only to the extent that they have been rationally demonstrated – is rejected in favor of a theory according to which truth can be found in opinion. Of course, the Western tradition since Plato had presupposed a strong distinction between truth and opinion. Just because someone has an opinion about something certainly doesn't mean that the opinion is correct. Indeed, when an opinion turns out to be true – that is, proven – it actually ceases to be a "mere" opinion and comes to be understood, instead, as a matter of fact. According to Zerilli, Arendt essentially rejects this line of thought, arguing instead that truth comes precisely out of the exchange of opinions and, more specifically, from the ability to see things from the other person's perspective. In this connection, Zerilli attributes to Arendt what she (Zerilli) calls the "paradox of truth." On the one hand, facts are contingent, not absolute; they are variable, and dependent on a point of view; they are subject to lies and distortions and all manner of error and misperception and are, as such, not compelling or incontestable in the way that scientific and rationalist models would suggest. They are, indeed, matters of opinion. On the other hand, this doesn't mean that facts are matters of mere preference or caprice. Rather, acknowledging truths to be true in some non-arbitrary sense is essential for politics. If we don't agree about the facts, then the possibilities for living together in intelligent and intelligible ways become problematic indeed. Hence the paradox: truth is real and necessary, but also elusive and unstable. Arendt seeks to overcome the paradox, according to Zerilli, by arguing that truth, properly understood, is embedded in a kind of common sense. The shared ability to look at things from the perspective of one's neighbors and fellow citizens allows one to see common tendencies in those various viewpoints, and to negotiate reasonable accommodations in the face of apparent disagreements. Such negotiation, moreover, is itself heavily dependent on the practice of rhetoric or persuasion, understood by Zerilli, following Arendt, to be the artful, and also distinctively political, activity of convincing one's fellow citizens – getting them to recognize – that one or another opinion really does reflect some kind of underlying consensus.

Going beyond Arendt, Zerilli seeks further to show that such a consensus reflects not simply a set of shared opinions or beliefs. Rather, it represents, as well, a variety of emotional attachments to those opinions. We have here an effort to rehabilitate the dimension of affect or feeling, understood as a crucial part of political judgment, properly understood. The Western tradition has long been skeptical not only of mere opinion but also, relatedly, of emotion or attitude or passion. Passions are irrational, haphazard, unjustified, and dangerous. They defy, as we say, rhyme or reason. As a result, we can't do whatever we feel like doing, and we can't let our judgments be governed by emotional impulses. Reason must control the passions if our actions and judgments are to be intelligible and defensible. This has long been the standard view, but Zerilli seeks strongly to modify it. In doing so, she invokes a burgeoning literature – an emergent tradition of "affect theory" – that focuses on the allegedly central and unavoidable role of emotions in understanding, explaining, and justifying human behavior.

According to that literature, much of what we do in life is largely a matter of "autonomic responses that are held to occur below the threshold of consciousness and cognition and to be rooted in the body."[9] Cognition is, to some degree, merely a reflection of physical drives, and this means that human action in general and human judgment in particular – including, presumably, political judgment – is non-intellectual, non-conceptual, and non-cognitive. Zerilli embraces this general standpoint, but again wants to have it both ways. That is, she wants to privilege affect without adopting an extreme non-cognitivism, and she claims to find a solution – a resolution of her own paradox – in the work of so-called ordinary language philosophy as represented perhaps pre-eminently by Ludwig Wittgenstein, one of the most important philosophers of the twentieth century. On Zerilli's account, Wittgenstein says that our engagement with the world is indeed automatic, unreflective, and non-intellectualistic. But it is also deeply cognitive insofar as we see things from the perspective of a particular way of life – a social or cultural mode of being – that we invoke unselfconsciously but that is nonetheless itself suffused with conceptuality and meaning. A way of life is, indeed, a structure of thoughts or cognitions. We learn or absorb those thoughts or cognitions as we become acculturated, often as we grow into adulthood, and this means that when we react immediately, automatically, and even emotionally to events and objects in the world, we nonetheless do so in a way that embodies those underlying conceptual or cognitive materials. Our affective attachment to particular opinions and judgments is always underwritten by a tacit structure of thought – a sense of truth – that places at least some significant constraints on what we can decide and how we can act.

Zerilli's account is useful in recognizing the limitations of Arendtian theory as standardly conceived, but it seems also to raise at least as many questions as it resolves. Thus, for example, she invokes the Socratic method as the model of an opinion-oriented rather than proof-oriented approach to truth, but in doing so she ignores or greatly underemphasizes the fact that Socrates actually employs a highly rationalistic mode of analysis designed to demonstrate beyond doubt the objective validity of some propositions and the objective falsity of others. The Socratic *elenchus* – the method of "refutation" – is precisely a matter of using the tools of logical analysis to prove or disprove the cogency of opinions and thereby to transform mere opinion into fact. Zerilli's relative inattention to the deep intellectualism of Socrates seems to be reflective, moreover, of a general pattern. Quoting Arendt, she says that by "comparing" a range of viewpoints we can arrive at opinions and judgments that are "more valid" than would otherwise be the case. We can learn, moreover, how to determine the degree to which those other viewpoints "reveal something about the world." We can discover their "blind spots" and can revise our own views so that they don't "distort reality." But, in saying such things, she fails to indicate exactly how we are reliably to compare, assess, and evaluate opinions and judgments in the absence of more or less explicit criteria that are independent of those opinions and judgments themselves; and it is hard to see how such opinion-independent criteria could involve anything other than a structure of cognitively rich and decidedly rationalistic principles having plausible claims to objectivity.

Zerilli goes on to criticize standard practices of rational and scientific inquiry for purporting to be able to discover "absolute" truth. But while science certainly presupposes what it seems nobody could deny, namely, that there is always a real fact of the matter out there that is being investigated, if only we can discover it, it is also in the very nature of science to undermine its own claims. Indeed, the basic idea of scientific progress is precisely to demonstrate that what was once thought by scientists to be true is in fact not true, and that progress of this kind is a constitutive, continuous, and perhaps never-ending feature of the scientific enterprise. More generally, the idea that rationality, proof, and objective, rule-based reasoning always involves claims to absolute knowledge is almost certainly false. For example, and as will be suggested in the next chapter, rational proof and objective demonstration are perfectly compatible with many forms of relativism; and the implications of this are crucial, for it means that the absence of absolute knowledge does not, in and of itself, justify or motivate an embrace of opinion, rhetoric, subjectivity, impulse, or emotion.

In the end, Zerilli claims that the focus of political judgment ought to be not on the rational evaluation of competing truth claims but, rather, on the distinctively political question of which issues or objects should be matters for public deliberation in the first place. Once again, though, it is hard to see how this is helpful; for presumably any decision as to what should or should not be a topic for political action will itself be a decision indeed and will require, as such, some effort at assessment and evaluation, some effort to weigh costs and benefits or to privilege one set of values or moral considerations over another, hence some effort to adjudicate among competing validity claims. Invoking opinion and affect doesn't seem sufficient to allow us to avoid the fundamental problem of arriving at defensible – indeed, rational – criteria upon which to base our judgments, political and otherwise.

4
Hermeneutics, Tacit Knowledge, and Neo-Rationalism

As we have seen, Zerilli invokes the ordinary language philosophy of Wittgenstein – above all, the notion that linguistic and other choices always occur internally to one or another specific way of life – in order to show how judgments can be both non-intellectualistic and cognitively substantial at the same time. Again, decisions that are immediate, automatic, and unexamined and that reflect, perhaps above all, attachments of an emotional nature may nonetheless be rooted in tacit commitments to some underlying set of cognitive materials, which can, in turn, be formulated in propositional terms, that is, as claims to knowledge. But, in making this argument, she refers as well to a second and rather different philosophical tradition, namely, the tradition of phenomenology that she associates with the contemporary philosopher Hubert Dreyfus, among others, and, through Dreyfus, the massively important early and mid twentieth century thinker, Martin Heidegger. Zerilli pursues this tradition primarily in considering the relationship between two kinds of knowledge, "knowing how" and "knowing that," an issue for which Heidegger is indeed relevant and that we will address a bit later on. But it is absolutely crucial to note that Heidegger's work is extremely important as well for a rather different strand of inquiry, one that focuses less on the question of immediate versus mediated kinds of knowledge and more on the more general problem of comprehension or understanding and that goes under the name of "hermeneutics." Heidegger himself places hermeneutics at the very center of his philosophy. Human beings are, on his account, fundamentally hermeneutic creatures; and while Zerilli does indeed talk at some length about the hermeneutic tradition – with respect, especially, to the writings of Hans-Georg Gadamer, one of Heidegger's most influential students – it is not clear that she exploits these materials as effectively as she might in pursuing her own theoretical agenda.

1

Hermeneutics is, roughly speaking, the science or art or practice of interpretation. That's a fairly nebulous and unhelpful observation in itself, but its concrete implications are easy enough to specify. If you say something to me – if you engage in what philosophers call a speech-act – presumably you are trying to convey some kind of meaning. My job as a listener and as a partner in conversation is to figure out just what that meaning is, that is, exactly what it is that you're trying to communicate. My job is to interpret your utterance. Usually this is pretty easy. If we speak the same language and share largely the same cultural background, then interpreting what you're saying will typically be straightforward indeed. Thus, if you're a competent speaker of English and you say, in English, that you like ice cream or that I should study for the exam or that the automobile is red, in each of these cases I am very likely to know quite well what you're talking about, assuming that I too am a competent speaker of English. This general pattern almost certainly describes, moreover, the vast majority of human interactions involving language. But it doesn't describe all of them. Indeed, it should be obvious that many situations are highly problematic in precisely these terms. For example, suppose you say that the Outback is red, and I don't know that an Outback is a particular kind of automobile; or suppose that I happen to live in a culture where there are no automobiles and that I've never even heard of such items; or suppose that you yourself don't distinguish things that are red from things that are orange, hence use the same word to refer to both. In all such circumstances, there will be a barrier to my understanding what you're saying, and this means that I face a problem of interpretation. In order to interpret your statement accurately that the Outback is red – to judge its meaning correctly – I have to find out what an Outback is, or find out what an automobile is, or find out how you happen to use the word red. It is easy enough to see, moreover, why problems of this kind are thought to be especially challenging when we are trying to understand statements made by someone who is either far removed from us in time or else far removed from us culturally. Indeed, correctly understanding the meaning of a text that was produced many centuries ago or a text that was produced in a very different and alien society is an inherently difficult business that often requires us to pay special attention to the very process of interpretation itself. What kinds of skills or tools or resources do we have at our disposal properly to see what, say, Plato or Aristotle is arguing, or to comprehend the poetry of the Han dynasty, or even to know what the daily press of present-day Baghdad is reporting? In this context, moreover, it should be clear that the problem of interpretation has perhaps special force when we're trying to translate expressions from one language to another. To be sure, translation is often quite straightforward. If you say in French "C'est un chien," we can easily agree that in German this means "Das ist ein Hund" and in English "That is a dog." In such cases, the interpretive challenges are trivial. But sometimes the peculiarities and subtleties of linguistic practice make it almost impossible fully to capture in one language the sense of what is being expressed in another. In cases of that kind, interpretation is apt to be an enormous challenge. But I would also suggest that such cases are actually examples of the more general problem of linguistic interpretation. For while the literature on hermeneutics does indeed emphasize the challenges of interpreting meaning across differences of time and culture, even the most straightforward instances of interpretation – for example, "I like ice cream" – have to be accounted for in theoretical terms. We need, in short, to understand how it is even possible to interpret meaning correctly and reliably.

Gadamer is arguably the foremost modern theorist of hermeneutics, and his work certainly has profound implications for the problem of judgment, even as Zerilli has formulated it.[1] His treatment of interpretation is rooted in a discussion of a specific range of kindred ideas or categories, which he himself calls the guiding concepts of humanism. These include notions of cultivation, tact, taste, common sense and, obviously most importantly for our purposes, judgment itself. Such concepts are, on his account, central to our own shared understanding of what it means to be a human being. Indeed, they are essential for making sense not only of our ability to comprehend linguistic materials but also for our ability intelligently to navigate – to judge correctly – the very world in which we live.

Cultivation – the German word is *Bildung* – refers to the processes by which individuals are "formed" into fully developed human beings who embody and embrace, more or less unselfconsciously, the dispositions, values, attitudes, practices, and mores of the culture to which they belong. To be cultivated is simply to be in the habit of behaving appropriately, of doing what one is expected to do in a given situation, of saying the right thing at the right time. Gadamer insists that this is very much a matter of knowledge – we *know* what is expected of us – but it is not the kind of knowledge that comes from science or logic or any other type of self-consciously systematic, theoretical inquiry. It is, rather, a matter of acquiring "prejudices," which Gadamer understands not at all in a pejorative sense but, quite on the contrary, in the very positive sense of having literally pre-judgments, that is, intuitive, generally unexamined, implicit notions of right and wrong, appropriate and inappropriate, suitable and unsuitable. Of course, such notions may well vary greatly from culture to culture. What is appropriate today in, say, France may not have been appropriate in France five hundred years ago and may not be appropriate today in Borneo. But all cultures without exception have their standards and their criteria of right and wrong, and all cultures seek to cultivate – to acculturate or socialize – their members.

How, then, does cultivation occur? If it is not a matter of science or logic or rational analysis, then how does one learn cultural expectations and mores? Gadamer's answer to this question is fundamental to his entire enterprise: all human beings, without exception, are deeply situated – embedded – in one or another social and cultural context, and one acquires one's prejudices simply by growing up alongside, observing, and interacting with one's parents, teachers, neighbors, friends, colleagues, and the like. One becomes cultivated in the same way that very small children learn their native languages, namely, through immersion, emulation, repetition, and absorption. Indeed, learning a language is itself part and parcel of becoming cultivated; and, while it is true that children often learn in school how to read and to use grammar correctly, such learning typically presupposes that those children already know how to speak the language very well. For Gadamer, a culture is a massively complex web of pre-judgments – an infinitely large though usually tacit system of truth claims – composing a structure of knowledge that most of us possess well in advance of the more consequential choices that we make and on the basis of which we therefore live our lives.

Thus, for example, one acquires *tact* – one learns to be tactful – as part of one's cultivation; and there is no algorithm, no structure of rational argument, no explicit, rule-based principle that justifies and explains what is tactful and what isn't. When we encounter someone who has acted without tact, we simply say something like "That just isn't done," and in such a circumstance there is usually no need – indeed, virtually no ability – to say exactly why this is so. It simply is; and so, we generally just do what we're supposed to do. Similarly, but rather more complexly, we situate *taste* within the parameters of culturally shared pre-judgments. We say of someone that he or she is a person of good taste – regarding, perhaps, cuisine or clothing or interior design – and this means that the individual has the ability to distill and embody cultural values in a way that other members of the culture will recognize and appreciate, again without being able to say exactly why. All of this, moreover, is rooted in the notion of *common sense*. We saw in the previous chapter how Arendt employs some such idea to describe the kinds of criteria upon which to distinguish good judgment from bad. We also encountered worries about her formulation, pertaining especially to the apparent vagueness and lack of specificity regarding the actual contents of common sense. It may be that Gadamer is attempting to show how such worries can be addressed. For him, common sense is not merely a kind of special device that we can employ or consult from time to time in order to assess the cogency of judgments; nor is it some type of ineffable and perhaps vaguely occult power of perception. Quite on the contrary, it functions substantively as nothing less than the very glue of society; for the commitments of common sense – the shared and collective understandings of how things in the world really are – are essentially constitutive of culture itself. They make a particular culture what it is and this means, among other things, that the content of common sense is not merely accessible but is, in fact, actually and routinely deployed by the vast majority of people who live and work in that culture. Again, the claims of common sense may vary greatly from culture to culture. It is a matter of debate as to whether universal truths exist and are discoverable; and as we will see, this turns out to be an important issue for Gadamer himself. But either way, the idea of hermeneutics, as he has formulated it, rests upon the notion of a common structure of cultural norms and intuitions – prejudices – that are absolutely constitutive of everyday social life as we know it, despite the fact that they are rarely if ever formulated in precise, scientific, rule-based terms. Indeed, one cannot prove the truth of common sense (here, Gadamer and Arendt are on the same page); for any effort at such a proof would itself be dependent on the very same structure of pre-judgment that underwrites common sense itself.

It is important to note the overdetermined nature of the argument. Understanding the meaning of cultivation, and of the other humanistic concepts, is, as we have seen, crucial to understanding what it means to be human. But we can understand cultivation itself – what it means – only if we are already cultivated, since it is through cultivation that meaning is to be accessed. The argument is circular. Gadamer is producing, in effect, a hermeneutics of hermeneutics, an interpretation of interpretation. His approach is, as such, an example of thought thinking itself, of the mind making explicit its own implicit operations; and on Gadamer's account, this kind of circularity is not at all vicious. Whereas circular arguments in science and logic utterly destroy the logico-scientific goal of generating objective proofs from, so to speak, the outside, hermeneutic circularity, as a form of internal self-discovery and self-evaluation, emerges as an unavoidable, defining, necessary, and highly productive feature of the interpretive enterprise itself.

All of this leads to a powerful and influential account of interpretation in particular and judgment – presumably including political judgment – in general. To interpret any kind of meaningful artifact, for example, an utterance, a written statement, a work of art, or even an intentional action, is to view it from the perspective of a shared "horizon" of understanding that is composed, as we have seen, of the collective prejudices or prejudgments of a culture. Such prejudices function jointly as a kind of filter or, perhaps, a structure of signification that imposes upon the object a set of culturally specific categories, including categories of evaluation as well as comprehension, and on the basis of which we can render the object intelligible. The meaning of the object is never simply inherent in the thing itself. Nothing in the world is self-interpreting. Rather, meaning is always constructed as, at most, a kind of negotiation between the object as we might imagine it to be independent of us and our interpretative resources. In a sense, then, to judge the meaning of an artifact – and, indeed, to judge pretty much anything – is a matter of discovering or uncovering the understanding of the thing that is already present, however unselfconsciously, in our common cognitive apparatus. It is a matter of making the implicit explicit, of turning our tacit pre-judgments into overt and expressed judgments. Formulated along these lines, judgments express nothing new. Or to be more specific, they add no new content to our account of things. What they do add, however, is a new kind of self-awareness. Our judgments bring our prejudices out into the open, and this is a non-trivial development, since a judgment that has been overtly expressed is now a judgment that is eligible for analysis, assessment, and critique, that is, eligible for another level of judgment – a judgment concerning our judgment – and so on in, again, a kind of unending circle.

Gadamer actually believes that much of this account is applicable to scientific as well as humanistic practice. His view is that there are literally no pure perceptions. This is to say that every observation – even including highly technical scientific observations, whether in the lab or in the field – is made from a particular perspective, and that the perspective is in no small measure determinative of our account of the thing itself. There is, in effect, no point of view outside of culture, no angle of vision that is not embedded in and imbued with cultural prejudice. All judgments are, in a very robust sense, products of socio-historical situations, and this means, among other things, that they resist, to one degree or another, the kind of external, objective processes of proof and demonstration that have traditionally – though in Gadamer's terms, falsely – been associated with science and logic. Gadamer is yet another theorist who denies that judgment, properly understood, can ever be "rationalistic" in the sense of following strict, rule-based, algorithmic procedures. Judgment is always a matter of interpretation understood as a process of decoding meanings, and this can never plausibly be reduced to a kind of external and self-standing calculus.

But judgment is also not non-cognitive. To the exact opposite, the prejudices upon which a culture is based obviously have real propositional content. Indeed, they compose virtually the entirety of propositional claims that are made about the world, internal to a particular cultural perspective, most of which are tacit and all of which constitute, collectively, a broad-based theory of reality, a metaphysics. This is Gadamer's solution to the basic problem that we encountered in Chapter 1 and that we have been exploring ever since, namely, how there can be a non-scientific and non-algorithmic concept of judgment that is nonetheless committed to the idea of rational truth. His solution is based on the claim that objective truth is always relative to a particular socio-historical situation; it is not transcendent in the sense of being culturally independent. But within the parameters of a particular culture itself, there always are, and must be, real and recognizable distinctions between propositions that are valid and those that are invalid, propositions that are correct and those that are incorrect, propositions that are true and those that are false.

2

It is plain that Gadamer rejects the standard view of judgment in science as the neutral and universally valid pursuit of independently objective claims about nature. Again, he insists that all observations are situated within culturally rich contexts and that a perspective external to any and all such contexts is simply unavailable to us. Interestingly, however, he also sharply distances himself from what he calls the "aesthetic hypothesis," something that he associates with Kantianism – though not necessarily with Kant himself – and that he sees as having been dominant in the modern world of artistic production and criticism. Indeed, a rejection of post-Kantian conceptions of art is clearly at the very core of his project. It is important for us to understand, then, in exactly what ways Gadamer's approach to art relates to that of Kant himself, for this has been, I believe, widely misconstrued.

As we saw, Kant views aesthetic judgment – of both art objects and natural objects – as a matter of reflective judgment, hence as a non-cognitive enterprise in which one necessarily claims to be making statements of universal validity even as one knows, or should know, that such claims cannot be proven or even materially supported by any kind of substantive argument or evidence. I would suggest, however, that this is not, strictly speaking, a theory of art at all. It is, rather, a theory of beauty (natural as well as artistic), and that's a very different thing. Indeed, it seems that Kant's account of beauty is perfectly compatible with many other ways of thinking about artistic experience and judgment. Post-Kantian writers on art often ignore this fact, but it is crucial in understanding what Gadamer has to say about aesthetics. For in his view, while beauty may or may not be an important part of an art object, the primary focus of artistic endeavor is very much elsewhere. Perhaps above all, art is a mode of communication in which a culture, through the agency of the painter or sculptor or author, uncovers and presents to itself one or more of the validity-claims upon which it is based. The goal of the artist is to express some truth about the world, with the understanding that any such truth will unavoidably reflect the standpoint of the culture in which the artist is operating. When Flaubert writes about Madame Bovary or when Monet paints a haystack or when Frank Capra makes a film about small-town America, the point is somehow to capture and articulate the truth of such things, as conceived, of course, by the culture itself. And indeed, this is largely why we read novels, look at paintings, watch films. Entertainment value aside, the underlying goal is not primarily to enjoy that ineffable and unexpected encounter with "purposiveness without purpose" that consti- tutes, in Kantian terms, the aesthetic experience. Our goal, rather, is to deepen and enrich our shared understanding of how things in the world are. It is doubtful that Gadamer would deny the possibility of having an aesthetic experience in the Kantian sense – that is, an experience of something beautiful – but doubtful, as well, that Kant would limit the function of art to the representation of beauty. Gadamerian art can certainly be beautiful and Kantian art can certainly have a theoretical agenda. But Gadamer does want to say that an undue emphasis on beauty inclines one to overlook or underestimate the constitutively discursive or cognitive features of artistic endeavor, hence to miss the very funda- mental truth-oriented role that such endeavor necessarily plays in virtually any cultural setting.

But how could we know that a novel or painting or film is adequately expressing the truth? Why should we think that the artist knows what he or she is talking about? In addressing such questions, Gadamer refers once more to the culturally situated practice of interpretation. There is, again, no rule or algorithm or scientific principle for deciding whether or not, say, *Madame Bovary* is telling us the truth about bourgeois married life in nineteenth-century France. But this doesn't mean that our judgment about that question is non-cognitive; for Gadamer wants to put great emphasis here on the humanistic and epistemological value of *recog- nition*. Flaubert's novel will be counted as a source of wisdom and insight, as having captured an important part of the truth, if the reader recognizes the plausibility of Flaubert's analysis, that is, if there's something about that analysis that rings a bell, that strikes a chord, that seems to resonate with the reader's own underlying if often only implicit intuitions about the truth of things. This process of recognition, moreover, can be based on nothing other than a kind of tacit understanding that is deeply rooted in the larger cultural apparatus that author and reader share. Just as the cultivated person, having absorbed and embraced, however unselfconsciously, the prejudices of the culture, will simply know what it means to act, say, tactfully, so will the deeply embedded reader simply understand – he or she will see – the degree to which Flaubert's novel captures and helps us comprehend some significant feature of reality.

In invoking the idea of recognition, Gadamer makes explicit reference to the ancient notion of *anamnêsis* or "recollection," and thereby refers us all the way back to Plato. In a wonderful and important dialogue called the *Meno*, Plato has Socrates pose the following very basic and very troubling question: if we want to know what something is and if we really and truly don't yet know what it is, how will we even be able to recognize it when we see it?[2] It is a thorny problem indeed, and Plato proposes what he believes to be the only intelligible solution. Since we actually do seem to learn new things all the time, it must be the case that our souls already "know" those things – indeed, they must already know pretty much everything there is to know – prior to any discovery that we might make. On such an account, learning new things is and can be nothing more than making our implicit knowledge explicit; and it is largely for this reason that Plato, through the literary character of Socrates, sees himself as a kind of philosophical midwife who discovers material that's already there, material that's already present within each of us, and simply helps us bring that material to the light of day. Gadamer is very much taken with such a notion, but his approach differs from Plato's in one important respect. Whereas Plato seems to think that our implicit knowledge is somehow inborn – something universal and inherent in all human beings, a kind of gift of the gods or of nature – Gadamer sees it, rather and more simply, as a product of cultivation. If, as we have seen, our sense of tact or taste or common sense is rooted in the conceptual apparatus – the prejudicial structure – of the culture in which we happen to find ourselves, then so too, and in exactly the same way, for the judgments we make regarding the quality and veracity of works of art. If we come to see that a particular work of art is telling us something that is both important and true, this is because it speaks to – it helps bring to the light of day – some number of implicit truth claims to which we, as cultivated individuals, are already deeply committed, if only unselfconsciously. In such a circumstance, we recognize something in the work of art that we recognize in ourselves; and for Gadamer, the great role of art in human affairs is precisely to act itself as a kind of midwife that helps us better understand those things that we already know, deep down.

The difference here between Plato and Gadamer might suggest that Plato is a universalist, Gadamer a relativist or cultural determinist. That's obviously right for Plato, but Gadamer's account is more complicated. For a central part of his argument involves what he famously calls the "fusion of horizons." In a sense, this simply refers to the very basic and ordinary process of everyday interpretation and judgment itself. If you say something and I interpret it correctly, that can happen only if your point of view is somehow making contact with – is overlapping or otherwise bound up with – mine. All interpretation occurs from one or another particular perspective; all interpretation is therefore hostage to the perspective of the interpreter; and even if you and I are very close to one another in cultural terms, it is still unavoidably the case that we will be looking at things from at least somewhat different angles since, if nothing else, our life experiences will inevitably have been at least somewhat different from one another. As a result, it is never possible, even in the most straightforward case, for me to be absolutely and entirely certain that my interpretation of what you've said is correct. But obviously this hardly means that we're entirely in the dark. We can ask one another questions, test hypotheses, search for evidence of common ground; indeed, these kinds of things occur all the time, routinely and successfully. Gadamer wants to say that intercultural engagement – hermeneutics across space and time – can happen in very much the same way. My understanding of an ancient text or of a text from a very different part of the world will always be fraught with uncertainty. Again, my judgment will necessarily reflect my own particular point of view. But we have resources – for example, historical, linguistic, and institutional forms of evidence – for engaging critically and overcoming interpretive challenges, and this suggests, in Gadamer's view, that the relativity of prejudicial structures, hence the perspectival nature of judgment itself, does not necessarily present an insuperable obstacle to the development of cross-cultural interpretations and representations that can plausibly, if provisionally, be accepted as valid.

3

Gadamer is not known for having produced a theory of specifically *political* judgment or, indeed, for having produced a political theory at all. But his approach very much resonates in the writings of any number of important and influential twentieth- and twenty-first-century political thinkers of various description. Interestingly, this includes at least some authors of consequence whose works rarely if ever mention Gadamer himself and who might not have even been familiar with or aware of his books and essays.

Michael Oakeshott, a major British political philosopher of, primarily, the post-war period, was Gadamer's almost exact contemporary, having been born in 1901, one year after Gadamer. His work emerges out of a century-long tradition of British idealism and British Hegelianism and, as such, reflects an intellectual genealogy that is sharply different from Gadamer's, whose writings are rooted in the German interpretive and phenomenological line of thought associated, variously, with Friedrich Schleiermacher, Wilhelm Dilthey, Friedrich Nietzsche, and, perhaps above all, Martin Heidegger. It is by no means clear, moreover, that Oakeshott was influenced in any direct way by Gadamer (nor Gadamer by Oakeshott). Nonetheless, their accounts of judgment are, in many ways, strikingly similar. This has not always been recognized by scholars. Oakesthott is widely viewed as a fairly typical – though untypically influential – mid-century political conservative and, thus, as a kind of latter-day Edmund Burke, though his debt to Hobbes is also well noted. This seems quite correct as far as it goes, but it ignores many of the deeper epistemological notions that are central to Oakeshott's thought and that pertain, above all, to the problem of political judgment.

Oakeshott's principal target is what he calls "rationalism in politics," the very idea of which he regards as a major category mistake and a dangerous one at that.[3] By rationalism, he understands a mode of thought that is formulaic, systematic, and confidently aimed at discovering objective truth. For a rationalist, the human mind is, or ought to be, a "finely tempered, neutral instrument." Of course, in criticizing such a mode of thought, Oakeshott qualifies as yet another theorist who vigorously rejects the rule-based, algorithmic, neutralist, aperspectival, and broadly scientistic understanding of political judgment that has its roots, as we have seen, in Plato. For Oakeshott, as for Arendt and others that we have encountered, politics, properly understood, is not at all a matter of proof or demonstration. Political or practical knowledge "cannot be formulated in rules." Indeed, when politics is conceived in purely calculative or "technical" terms, the result is apt to be one or another variety of ideologically driven and brutally repressive totalitarianism, as exemplified in mid-century by the Nazi pursuit of (pseudo) scientific theories of racial purity and the Stalinist pursuit of so-called scientific socialism. Like Arendt, Oakeshott sees politics and political judgment as *sui generis*, not at all reducible to any kind of scientific, economic, or even philosophical manner of thinking. But unlike Arendt, he conceives of politics not in terms of persuasive speech, free and spontaneous action, or courageous, audacious, and originary enterprise, and there can be no doubt that he would strongly disavow Arendt's emphasis on natality or innovation. Rather, politics is, for Oakeshott, essentially a matter of "attending to arrangements." The arrangements in question are the governing habits and practices of a particular political society, and attending to them means thinking carefully, modestly, and pragmatically about repairing defects or infelicities in institutions and procedures whose overall merit is reflected in the simple fact that, to one degree or another, they have stood the test of time.

In elaborating such an approach, however, Oakeshott refers to what he calls, at one point, the "pursuit of intimations." When we attend to arrangements, we are necessarily making judgments and decisions about what does and doesn't need to be reformed, and how; and to pursue intimations is to discover what is already implicit in those arrangements – to uncover their underlying and usually tacit logic – and to use those discoveries to judge and decide how to make modifications in actual practice that would be more in keeping with that underlying logic. It is to ensure that political activity is faithful to the internal commitments – moral, empirical, metaphysical – that are already present, if hidden, in our political way of life and that, as such, reflect the larger cultural traditions of which we are a product.

Oakeshott provides a striking, if also highly controversial, example in the case of women's suffrage. In his view, the extension of the vote to women in the United Kingdom (and presumably elsewhere) should not have reflected, and in actual fact did not reflect, the influence of an abstract, disembodied, universalistic doctrine of human rights or even of feminism. Rather, it represented a culture's coming to realize that its own routine practices and experiences already presupposed, in thousands of ways large and small, the moral and intellectual equality of women with men. The fact that women were not allowed to vote was a kind of cultural self-contradiction, and the official enfranchisement of women was thus essentially a matter of enshrining and effectuating widely shared intuitions, beliefs or intimations.

The connection here with Gadamer should be obvious. Oakeshott's pursuit of what a culture intimates seems largely to be an inquiry into what Gadamer calls the prejudgments or prejudices that compose the foundations of a culture. Whereas the rationalism that Oakeshott criticizes utterly rejects prejudice, Oakeshott himself, like Gadamer, very much embraces it (though his terminology is generally different). Like Gadamer, he says that genuine practical knowledge – good judgment, political wisdom, interpretive insight – cannot be formally taught or learned; it can only be "imparted and acquired." And like Gadamer, he indicates that that which is imparted is "already there," that is, already present and available in a culture's shared understanding of how things in the world really are. What persons of good judgment possess is, above all, the common sense of their own socio-cultural world, and they are in possession of this simply in virtue of being part of that particular world, that is, being deeply embedded in it on an everyday basis.

But Oakeshott's writings also present a particularly important and challenging problem. It is a problem, moreover, that is present as well, though perhaps rather less evident, in Gadamer's work. Specifically, in deploying common sense, in invoking cultural prejudgments or prejudices, in educing that which has been intimated by our way of life, how can we be sure that we have gotten it right? What can be done actually to justify judgments and other claims, even assuming that those things are culturally specific? More basically, what is the process – what are the intellectual or cognitive operations – by which one discovers the implicit claims and principles of the larger conceptual and metaphysical apparatus upon which one relies? Or again: exactly where do we find common sense and what authorizes and supports our claim to have been faithful to it? It is here that Oakeshott is candid and explicit in a way that Gadamer perhaps is not. In Oakeshott's phrase, "there will always remain something of a mystery about how a tradition of political behavior is learned …." Or as he says in one of his earliest writings, a brilliant if now largely ignored book entitled *Experience and its Modes*, "[i]t is not the clear-sighted, not those who are fashioned for thought and the ardours of thought, who can lead the world. Great achievements are accomplished in the mental fog of practical experience. What is farthest from our needs is that kings should be philosophers."[4] Here is a bracing and unvarnished statement of an anti-intellectualist or, at least, non-intellec-tualist account of practical wisdom or political judgment. Political judgment is not a matter of rigorous and explicit propositional analysis; on the contrary, it emerges out of a "mental fog." In this sense, Oakeshott seems to be very much on the same page with Arendt. Yet, as we have seen, Oakeshott, like Gadamer (and like the Arendt that Zerilli seeks to present), does not at all want to be understood as a non-cognitivist. The resources of culture and common sense out of which political judgment emerge are literally loaded with cognitive content, that is, with substantive claims about reality. So the problem seems clear: how can it be that our access to cognitive content is not itself primarily a matter of cognition, at least as understood in the usual, intellectualistic sense as involving discourse, analysis and the specification and justification of propositions? How can a theory of political judgment be significantly and decidedly cognitivist on the one hand and determinedly non-intellectualistic on the other? How does a foggy mind – a mind presumably unguided by systematic rational argumentation – hit upon and confidently embrace substantive propositions about how things in the world are? What is it that reliably justifies such propositions?

4

The problem becomes, if anything, even more perplexing if we consider other, seemingly quite different traditions of thought, including specifically political traditions, that pursue Gadamerian strategies – even if, like Oakeshott, they do so without explicitly invoking Gadamer himself. A good example is provided by certain influential late twentieth century debates in the philosophy of law. In a series of important and highly provocative essays, Stanley Fish presents a theory of legal interpretation – a theory about how we judge the meaning of laws – that insists on the central role of what we have been calling prejudgments or prejudices, but does so without addressing, much less resolving, the central question of cognitivism and non-intellectualism.

Fish's work is rooted in a broad account of the Anglo-American common law process of adjudication that had been brilliantly encapsulated somewhat earlier in a canonical study by Edward Levi entitled *An Introduction to Legal Reasoning.*[5] According to Levi, laws are not self-interpreting. If they were, judges would not be necessary. But judges are necessary, and this is largely because every case before the bar is in some sense unique. Each individual case is likely to present circumstances and issues that are distinctive, meaning specifically that their facts are inevitably different, to one degree or another, from those of cases that have been decided before. The job of the judge is, in part, to decide for any particular case exactly how it is different from and similar to previously decided cases, and thereby to determine which previously established legal principles apply to the instant case and which do not. But as Levi suggests, there seems to be no predetermined rule – no algorithm or formula or strict calculus – for doing this. The process is, and can only be, as we say, a matter of interpretation or judgment.

Of course, and as always, the problem is to discover what this really means and how it occurs. Fish addresses the issue by pursuing an analogy, suggested by the prominent legal theorist Ronald Dworkin, between the interpretation of law and the interpretation of literature. Fish himself is principally a scholar of literature, specializing in, among other things, medieval English poetry (though he has also taught in law schools). In a provocative and controversial essay entitled "How to Recognize a Poem When You See One" he describes an experiment that he once conducted in a course he was teaching on medieval poetics.[6] One day, before his students arrived for class, he put on the blackboard a brief list of six contemporary literary critics – their last names only – that constituted the weekly reading assignment for another, entirely different course. When the medieval poetics students arrived, he told them that the material on the board – the list of names – was a medieval poem and asked them to interpret it. Having no inkling that the list was in fact a class assignment rather than a poem, the students proceeded jointly to produce a literary analysis that was sophisticated, detailed, complex, and erudite. One of the contemporary authors on the list was named Jacobs while another was named Rosenbaum, and Fish recounts that:

> Jacobs was explicated as a reference to Jacob's ladder, traditionally allegorized as a figure for the Christian ascent to heaven. In this poem, however, or so my students told me, the means of ascent is not a ladder but a tree, a rose tree or rosenbaum. This was seen as an obvious reference to the Virgin Mary who was often characterized as a rose without thorns, itself an emblem of the immaculate conception.

One might conclude from this that Fish had succeeded in duping his students, and that he was perhaps ridiculing, in the process, the very kinds of analytic strategies that he had been teaching them. (Indeed, one might also guess that the students, upon finding out the truth, would have felt at least a little embarrassed, even humiliated, or perhaps angry.) But Fish's position is not this at all. He argues that the students, in analyzing the "poem," were simply demonstrating the fact that they were part of an "interpretive community," that all interpretation and judgment occurs internally to one or another such community, and that communities of interpretation have substantial leeway in determining how texts and other interpretable items should be understood. Fish seems to suggest that there was in fact nothing wrong with the students' analysis. They were faithfully employing the analytic techniques that they had learned from Fish himself, and if they concluded that the list was a poem, then Fish seems happy actually to accept that judgment. The "poem" is indeed a poem. Of course, this suggests a most radical kind of relativism. Fish is saying, in effect, that all of our judgments are made internal to one or another community of interpretation (few if any people live their lives outside of some such community), all of our judgments are therefore hostage to and parasitic on one or another manner of thinking, and any such manner of thinking has a great deal of leeway in interpreting the objects before it. If a list of the last names of living authors can be interpreted as a poem, then it is a bit hard to see how interpretations are in any way limited or constrained by the supposedly independent facts of the world out there. Anything can be interpreted as pretty much anything, provided only that interpretations are faithful to the theories and analytic tools of the interpretive community within which one is operating.

The legal theorist Dworkin seeks to push back against such an approach by using another literary example – a purely hypothetical one – in order to show that interpretations are and must be limited and constrained in important ways by features of the external object.[7] He imagines a group of authors who have chosen jointly to write a novel. Each author will write one chapter, and the chapters will be written seriatim, meaning that the second chapter will be written only after the first chapter has been completed, the third after the second, and so on. Dworkin's contention is that the author of the last chapter will have comparatively little freedom in composing that chapter, and certainly far less than the author of the first chapter, since the last chapter must reflect and be consistent with all of the chapters that preceded it. Those chapters will, in effect, sharply limit and constrain what the author of the last chapter can reasonably do. But Fish vigorously denies this.[8] In his view, Dworkin's account simply reflects the prejudices of one particular interpretive community – a community that views prose narrative in rather traditional, linear terms – and ignores thereby any number of other possible literary perspectives, some of which might indeed leave the last author virtually as free as the first in composing what would count as a "fitting" conclusion to the novel.

There are certainly many questions to be raised about the plausibility of Fish's overall approach. For example, even if he's correct in saying that the author of the last chapter of the novel would have a great deal of latitude in writing that chapter, far more than what Dworkin had supposed, surely it is necessarily the case that whatever gets written there will in some way be reflective of – will somehow have to register the impact of – all the previous chapters, if only to reject their (merely apparent) implications. This is simply to say that the force of the last chapter, and the decisions that the author will have made in composing it, cannot escape the fact that it is indeed the last chapter in a book that comprises all the others; and this means that the last author will indeed face at least some non-trivial limitations and constraints that will be different from those faced by the first author. As to the assignment/poem involving Jacobs, Rosenbaum, and the other names of contemporary literary critics, even if Fish wishes to insist that it really is a poem – perhaps arguing from the perspective of an interpretive community that views poetry as being produced in all kinds of ways and from all kinds of motivations – it is hard to see how the artifact in question could plausibly be understood as a *medieval* poem in the specific sense of something actually written in the Middle Ages. If Fish's students insist that the poem, if it is a poem, was written eight hundred years ago, then they are simply and unambiguously wrong about that.

It should be noted that the account that Fish provides of his own experiment is itself deeply problematic. If it is true that his students were part of an interpretive community the principles of which included, importantly, elaborate and sophisticated strategies and techniques for analyzing poems, it is certainly also true that the very same interpretive community would have allowed or, indeed, required those students to understand, among many other things, the difference between a poem and an assignment, the difference between something composed in the late twentieth century as opposed to, say, the eleventh, the difference between a medieval poet and a modern literary critic, and so on. Indeed, the students in the class were not just students in the class, and the larger interpretive community of which they were a part certainly included any number of ordinary claims about time and authorship that would have ruled out as incoherent the possibility that the assignment was a poem.

But it seems that the principal problem with Fish's account is, again, a certain failure to describe adequately in detail the actual process – the mental operation – by which interpretation occurs. The problem is crucial. For if judgment in general and political judgment in particular denotes, in the end, a certain intellectual faculty, a quality of mind, a character of thought, then we need to have a pretty good idea of just what that is. Exactly how do good judges do what they do and how does one learn to do it?

5

Yet another hermeneutically oriented approach that seeks to address such questions has been formulated by Alessandro Ferrara. In actual fact, Ferrara seeks fairly strongly to distance himself from Gadamer and explicitly relies heavily on Kant. For him, political judgment – and judgment in general – is best captured by the Kantian notion of reflective judgment, as we have described it above. However, Ferrara also insists on a particular kind of reflective judgment that is, unlike Kant's, "oriented," i.e., deeply rooted in and hostage to a type of shared social experience that provides a degree of guidance, control, or limitation that would otherwise be lacking. This is to say that reflective judgment is not entirely subjective or non-cognitive; it is not utterly unmoored. Rather, it is tethered to some set of considerations according to which any judgment, properly formulated, may be understood as expressing universal claims. In this respect, then, the account seems rather Gadamerian. But at the same time, Ferrara also wants to reject the more robust hermeneutic claims to knowledge. Whereas Gadamer says that our judgments embody and represent a shared, substantive understanding of how things in the world really are – internal, of course, to a particular socio-historical horizon – Ferrara essentially denies this. In effect, he wants to find a "third way" that resides between Kantian non-cognitive subjectivism on the one hand and hermeneutical socially located objectivism on the other.

He claims to find a model for such a third way in a particular kind of aesthetic theory according to which any work of art is to be judged according to standards that are internal to, and unique to, the particular work itself. Any such work has a certain coherence, an integrity, a unifying quality that gives it its distinctive identity. These are the features that make the work what it is; and a cogent analysis or interpretation of that work – a good judgment – is one that recognizes and reveals precisely those features. To judge accurately a work of art is to make claims about it that capture its special, individual spirit and character. Such an account presupposes that the aesthetic integrity of a work of art – its "well-formedness" – does not depend on fulfilling some kind of external rule, idea, or principle. Rather, each particular work of art is "universal in its very singularity.... [I]ts rule holds for one case only, but exactly in that it is universal, in the sense that it is the only law that should have been followed in its making."[9] If you have grasped the work's singularity, you've grasped its meaning.

Having outlined this aesthetic model, Ferrara then seeks to apply it to the problem of moral and political judgment. Here, however, the criteria for judgment involve considerations that pertain to the character and identity not of a work of art but of an action, of the actor him- or herself, and of the actor's relevant situation. Specifically, Ferrara's emphasis is on "self-realization or progress in self-realization or progress toward an authentic relation with oneself, where the expression 'authentic relation of the self with itself' designates an optimal congruence of identity with itself."[10] Roughly, a judgment is a good one if it captures – if it is "congruent" or consistent with – the character of the thing being judged as it pertains to the individuals involved in the judged enterprise. A sense of the identity of the situation in question thus provides a type of guideline that restricts the kind of total freedom that would be associated with subjective non-cognitivism without embracing the (putatively) confining metaphysics of traditional hermeneutics.

In pursuing such an account, Ferrara relies, as do Kant and Arendt, on a notion of *sensus communus*. But although he strives to distinguish his particular formulation from that of the others – the *sensus communus*, for Ferrara, pertains distinctively to wisdom about what conduces to human flourishing or authenticity – it is not at all clear that this solves the fundamental epistemological problem. One would guess that ideas and claims about authenticity and flourishing would themselves either be rooted in socio-cultural prejudgments, as hermeneuticians suggest, or be as insubstantial and ungrounded as any kind of Kantian aesthetic proposition. It is hard to see how it could be otherwise. In effect, then, one might well doubt whether Ferrara has indeed found a genuine third way.

To the degree that this is correct, the most fundamental questions remain unanswered. Indeed, it seems that we are brought all the way back to the original problem as outlined by Plato and Aristotle; and as we have seen, it is a problem that has become increasingly defined in terms of the relationship between non-intellectualist and cognitivist views of how humans meaningfully think about the world. As such, it motivates us to consider in some detail the distinction between what philosophers have come to call "knowing how" and "knowing that."

6

In a major work of modern analytic philosophy entitled *The Concept of Mind*, Gilbert Ryle argues that there are at least two very different senses in which we say of an individual that he or she knows something.[11] On the one hand, we know of certain propositions either that they are true or false, which is to say that we *know that* something is (or is not) the case. We know *that* a molecule of water is composed of two hydrogen atoms and one oxygen atom. We know *that* Germany invaded Belgium in 1940. We know *that* Gilbert Ryle wrote a book entitled *The Concept of Mind*. Propositions are statements about the world that link grammatical subjects to grammatical predicates and, thereby, say about some particular thing in the world that it has (or doesn't have) a certain particular feature or character; and to know that something is the case always presupposes that one's knowledge can indeed be stated in propositional form.

On the other hand, we also say of someone that he or she knows *how* to ride a bicycle, or knows *how* to recognize a face, or knows *how* to distinguish a major seventh chord from a dominant seventh chord; and it is a central thrust of Ryle's argument to insist that this kind of knowledge is fundamentally not a matter of propositions. To be sure, knowing how to ride a bicycle does imply knowledge of certain propositions. For example, it implies knowledge of the proposition that a bicycle is a mode of transportation having two wheels and that it is propelled by pushing down on pedals. It may even imply knowledge of the proposition that riding a bicycle generally requires you to sit down in the saddle. But such propositions are not sufficient to give one the requisite know-how; if you know those things, that doesn't at all mean that you know how to ride a bicycle. Indeed, there's a sense in which knowing how to ride a bicycle – the kind of thing that children learn through trial and error – doesn't seem to be even expressible in propositional terms. At the very least, it is clear that few people who know how to ride a bicycle have ever articulated in a systematic way any kind of propositional explanation as to why they can do it rather than, say, fall over. They just *know how* to do it. When they actually ride a bicycle, they simply ride it; they don't think about it. It is not that they don't give it a second thought; in the typical case, they don't seem to give it any thought at all.

Prior to Ryle, philosophers seem generally to have believed that knowing how must be rooted in knowing that. The standard view was that the exercise of a skill like riding a bicycle – or thousands upon thousands of other skills that compose a very large portion of ordinary human endeavor – requires some kind of prior consideration of one or more propositions. Ryle explicitly refers to this as an intellectualist account. According to such an account, skillful know-how reflects some kind of more or less self-conscious thought process – a cognitive or reflective analysis and assessment – that brings factual knowledge claims to bear on the relevant practical task. For Ryle, this is plainly incorrect. He notes, as a purely phenomenological matter, that much or most of the time we do what we do without any such prior consideration. Again, we simply get on the bicycle and ride; and with respect to bicycle riding and countless other practical activities, it is obvious that we often do this very skillfully indeed, and that self-conscious thought doesn't seem necessary or even especially helpful in becoming more skillful. Ryle therefore urges a sharply non-intellectualist understanding of know-how.

We need to be crystal clear about what is philosophically at stake here. Consider three different things that we "do" in ordinary life. The first is that we learn about the chemical composition of a molecule of water. The second is that we open a door by turning the doorknob. The third is that we breathe. Surely we will want to say that the first of these is, indeed, intellectualistic, a prototypical case of knowing that. Our knowledge that water is composed of two parts hydrogen and one part oxygen is explicit and self-conscious knowledge of a proposition. We will just as certainly want to say that the third of these – breathing – is purely automatic, something that our body does on its own, so to speak, and therefore is utterly and completely non-intellectualistic. Breathing just happens; it is something we rarely think about as it is occurring. The problem, however, is with the second case, the case of opening the door. In the vast majority of circumstances, we do this without thinking about it. We don't say to ourselves anything about the function of doors, about the method of operating a doorknob, about the actual mechanics of doorknobs, and so on. We simply open the door; and in view of this, Ryle and those who follow him want to say that opening a door is non-intellectualistic. But at the same time, it also seems nonetheless completely and utterly different from the case of breathing. Breathing is, in a sense, not really something that one *does* at all; opening the door plainly is. So if opening the door is non-intellectualistic, it seems to be so in a way that's very different from the non-intellectualist fact of breathing. The question is to figure out exactly what that difference might be.

If these issues seem distant from the problem of political judgment, I would suggest that they're not. In fact, I believe that they are central. Notice, for example, that Plato's discussion of a knack, as described in Chapter 1, is pretty much exactly the description of a kind of non-intellectualist know-how. A knack is something that does not and cannot give an account of itself, and it is precisely such a notion that Plato vigorously rejects as a description of political judgment. With respect to political judgment, then, Plato is a radical intellectualist. And the post-Platonic history of the theory of judgment represents, one might say, basically an on-going struggle to determine exactly how political action might be non-intellectualistic in a way that's like opening a door or riding a bicycle – something that we do, something that is not reducible to any kind of explicit propositional calculus, but something that is not like breathing or the blinking of the eyes or even the scratching of an itch. All of this, then, restates in modern terms the agenda that we have been pursuing all along, namely, to try to understand how judgment actually takes place such that things like riding a bicycle, opening the door or displaying practical wisdom in politics can be, at one and the same time, both non-intellectualistic and deeply cognitive.

7

It is a challenging agenda indeed and, in the face of it, recent scholarship appears largely to have given up on the cognitive pole altogether, embracing a fairly thorough-going non-intellectualism and non-cognitivism à la Ryle (and, in a different way, Arendt, *pace* Zerilli), but now with a distinctive twist that involves a special focus on the functioning of the human body itself. Recall, along these lines, the specific language used by *New York Times* columnist David Brooks in the passage with which this book began. The person of good judgment, he says, has, above all, a particular "feel" for what works; and other authors, as we have seen, talk about judgment as a kind of "sense." Such formulations employ, I would suggest, the metaphoric language of the body; to feel or to sense is, in the standard case, a physical kind of thing.

In the recent scholarly literature, an emphasis on the body sometimes takes the form of a neo-Heideggerian conception that emphasizes the central role in human life of "embodied coping." According to that conception, our lives are filled with an unending series of practical tasks – like opening a door – and in the face of such tasks it is common for our bodies simply to take over. When I see the doorknob, my arm and hand do what they've done for years and more or less on their own, without cognitive content and without anything that would count as an explicit instruction from me. If such a formulation seems insufficient to distinguish human animals from non-human ones, or insufficient to distinguish opening a door from breathing, another, related approach has been to try to avoid this consequence, or at least soften it, by emphasizing the role of peculiarly human affect or emotion. As we have seen, some such focus is embraced at least in part by Zerilli, and the basic idea is that practical activity is, and indeed ought to be, driven or strongly influenced by our feelings, for example, our desire for or aversion to certain things in the world; and while non-human animals are certainly also creatures of desire and aversion, the range and complexity of human emotion is infinitely greater – it seems, for example, that humans but not animals can have desires about desires – and this means that the analysis of emotion-based human judgment is apt to be an unusually rich subject in itself. In pursuing this general line of thought, moreover, many contemporary non-intellectualist notions advert as well to the astonishing developments in modern neuroscience, sometimes to justify their affect-oriented descriptions of practical activity and sometimes, it seems, to suggest that an adequate, scientific justification is likely to be just around the corner.[12]

Affect-oriented theories are said to be attractive in at least three ways. First, they purport to recognize and celebrate the "whole person" and reject, thereby, the long-standing tendency of such otherwise disparate philosophers as Plato and Kant to see humans as sharply divided or even schizophrenic creatures whose rational faculties are constantly at war with their instincts and appetites. Second, they help delegitimize historically dominant but deeply scurrilous gender stereo-types according to which level-headed, objective, rational males are best suited to govern while emotional, impulsive, unreliable females are better suited to life in the private realm – though the line between rejecting such stereotypes as empirically absurd and embracing but radically re-evalu-ating them (e.g., emotion is a good thing) can be a tricky one to negotiate. But third, and perhaps most important, emotivist views are presented as simply more accurate or realistic accounts of how judgments actually occur, both within and outside of politics. Citizens in the voting booth, legislators in parliament, judges on the bench, presidents or prime ministers – all such individuals, despite what they may claim, make decisions that fundamentally reflect their own desires, biases, personal predilections, and gut instincts. Such factors compose the real fundamentals of political choice and judgment; anything above or beyond that is largely window-dressing, a structure of post-hoc rationalization designed principally to attach a veneer of objective legitimacy to what are, at base, matters of subjective preference.

The concern here should be obvious. A non-intellectualist, affect-oriented approach threatens the very idea of distin-guishing good judgments from bad. If everything is, in the last analysis, a matter of how one feels, then on what basis shall we say that a certain set of feelings or emotions is better than another? Indeed, a thoroughgoing affect-oriented approach would have to acknowledge, on its own account, that any comparative assessment and evaluation of emotionally based judgments must itself be an emotionally based judgment, and this seems unavoidably to produce an infinite regress. If authentic feelings are to be given pride of place, then who is to say – and on what basis – that one set of feelings is more legitimate or more valid or more true or more useful than another? Indeed, what could any such claim mean? Notice, moreover, that the moment we insist that someone is wrong to feel a certain way – for example, you may feel that the sun revolves around the earth but you're wrong, or your feelings of anger toward your opponent are likely to do more harm than good – we begin immediately to move sharply away from affect or emotion and into the realm of reason, argument, rationality, and objective truth.

Problems such as these may help explain the recent emergence of a neo-rationalist conception of political judgment.[13] Such a conception runs exactly counter to the non-intellectualist and non-cognitivist tendencies of affect theory, though it does seek to incorporate important insights from (inter alia) hermeneutic, phenomenological, and ordinary language traditions. The neo-rationalist argues, above all, that non-intellectualist theories of whatever kind – including both the Rylian/Heideggerian emphasis on knowing how or embodied coping and the emotivist or affect-oriented account of judgment – seriously misunderstand the very idea of intellectualism and rationality. That misunderstanding, moreover, can be traced specifically to three serious mistakes.

According to non-intellectualists, intellectual content – for example, knowledge of propositions – can be in play only if it is explicit. When Ryle claims that know-how frequently does not involve prior consideration of propositions, this means that persons engaged in practical activity often do not actually articulate, to themselves or to anyone else, any set of beliefs that might be connected with that activity. The activity is simply performed; and the absence of explicitly articulated propositions is taken as evidence that beliefs or truth claims are not especially important or necessary in performing the action itself. But beliefs can be implicit. We can be and indeed are committed to propositions or truth claims – lots of them – without ever having articulated them.

I am committed, for example, to the proposition that a violin is smaller in physical size than the Atlantic Ocean. It is possible, indeed likely, that neither I nor anyone else has ever actually articulated that proposition. And yet, I know it and believe as certainly as I know and believe anything, and have done so long before I wrote these sentences. Even though it is only an implicit belief, it is clearly a belief that I hold and that informs my actions. Of course, one is tempted to observe of such a proposition that it simply "goes without saying." But this is only to demonstrate that intellectual content need not be explicit in order to be operative and important; and it should be apparent that the number of implicit, tacit, unarticulated beliefs to which any normal person is committed is staggeringly large.

Second, non-intellectualists suggest that for intellectual content to be in effect it must be non-immediate. Ryle's claims about prior consideration suggest a picture according to which I stop and think before performing an action; and since a great deal of action seems not to be performed in that way – I generally don't stop and think before opening the door – such action looks to be non-cognitive or non-intellectualistic. But it is hard to see why propositional knowledge – knowing that – couldn't be invoked more or less immediately, even instantly. Consider Wittgenstein's famous case of the duck/rabbit. A drawing, if looked at in one way, appears to depict the head of a duck (it has two large oblong shapes that seem to be the duck's bill) and, if looked at in another way, the head of a rabbit (the same two shapes now look like the ears of a rabbit). If you see it as the drawing of a duck, then you can't see it is as the drawing of a rabbit – until, suddenly, you do. And when you do finally see it as a rabbit, this seems simply to happen automatically, without reflection, analysis, or argument, hence without time for the prior consideration that the intellectualist might require. But surely recognizing that the rabbit is also a duck would be impossible without all kinds of propositional knowledge regarding ducks and rabbits, for example, knowing that rabbits often have large floppy ears. The fact that I know that rabbits often have large floppy ears is essential to my recognizing the rabbit in the drawing, even if I don't actually take the time to say to myself or anyone else that often rabbits have large floppy ears. The issue here actually raises complicated questions about time and cognition. When I see that the duck is also a rabbit, am I actually consulting and invoking – "considering" – my store of propositional knowledge, only doing so with extraordinary speed? Or am I not actively considering it at all, but simply judging in an immediate flash? It is a difficult question. But in either case, my awareness that the duck can also be seen as a rabbit – my knowing how to see it as both – is and can only be rooted in a complexly cognitive and substantively rich structure of thought according to which I know intellectually that ducks and rabbits have and are constituted by certain physical features. Propositional content can be deeply and profoundly in play even if judgment and action occur, or seem to occur, without evident reflection.

Finally, the non-intellectualist thinks that intellectual engagement is such only if it is in some sense detached. To approach a problem or a task cognitively or thoughtfully is necessarily to take a step back from the problem or task and examine it, so to speak, from the outside. It is to engage in a separate process of analysis; for without this, how could one say that the task has been the product of intellectual or propositional engagement? And the non-intellectualist will point out that many practical tasks seem to be performed without any distancing at all. In a much cited example, the great French phenomenologist Maurice Merleau-Ponty offers the hypothetical case of a soccer player who is dribbling the ball and bearing down on the goal, intent on beating his or her defender so as to shoot the ball into the net. According to Merleau-Ponty, the player, at that very moment, is so intent on the action – so involved in the know-how of the situation, so lost in the circumstance itself, in the heat of battle – that he or she is not even aware that all of this is occurring in a game of soccer. The player's total involvement means that he or she cannot be thinking about, hence cannot be conscious of, the fact that he or she is playing soccer. But this seems deeply unconvincing. Consider, for example, a thought experiment in which we suddenly stop the action on the soccer pitch and ask the soccer player what game is being played. Surely the player would answer immediately, instantly, and without the slightest evidence of reflective thought that the game is soccer. Indeed, if there would be any delay at all, it would likely

occur only if the soccer player were to look at us incredu-
lously, as if we had asked a ridiculous question. It seems
absurd to deny that such a player is constantly well aware of
the fact that he or she is playing soccer, and also well aware
of any number of other things involving, say, the basic rules
of soccer; and it seems certain that all of this constitutes a
vast system of propositions or truth claims or knowing-that
without which the know-how would be unintelligible and
to which the practitioner has something like instant and
undetached access.

The neo-rationalist theory of judgment argues that
practical activity, including political activity, is typically
underwritten by propositional claims, many or most of
which are implicit and which compose, collectively, the
essential character of the action itself as an embodiment
and manifestation of judgment. An action and the judgment
that informs it is, in short, determined by its constitutive
beliefs. As Gadamer indicates, those beliefs reflect a shared
structure of metaphysical presupposition; they are embedded
in culture, and this means that practical judgment and
activity is intelligible only and exclusively as a manifestation
of a society's way of life. But neo-rationalism adds to this a
series of insights derived from a very different philosophical
perspective, namely, a late twentieth and early twenty-first
century line of thought associated with so-called analytic
philosophers including, among many others, P. F. Strawson,
Hilary Putnam, Donald Davidson, Robert Brandom, and
John McDowell. Despite their many differences, such writers
agree that human engagement in the world always presupposes a more or less common conceptual and theoretical
apparatus that is in some sense prior to our encounter with
the world and that provides materials on the basis of which
we impose upon the world some kind of intelligible order.
As with hermeneutic theory, these analytic philosophers
argue that the mind functions more as a lamp than a mirror.
It doesn't merely or even mainly reflect but, rather, actively
organizes the material of the world as that material appears
to us. But such authors also emphasize what hermeneuticians
tend to ignore or underplay, namely, that any conceptual or
theoretical apparatus – any system of prejudgments – will
be a system indeed. It will compose, at least by aspiration, a

coherent structure of propositions, that is, propositions that are rationally consistent with one another. One implication of this, then, is that when someone offers a proposition, say, a proposition about which public policy proposal is best, it can and should be evaluated primarily in terms of the degree to which it is in fact consistent with the larger body of propositions of which the conceptual apparatus is composed. To the degree that a particular truth claim is contradicted by that larger body of propositions, it will be ruled out as incoherent. Indeed, truth claims are in fact true – judgments are valid – just insofar as they pass this test of coherence. The process is highly intellectualistic, indeed rationalistic. Propositions are assessed on the basis of strict rational criteria according to which a judgment is acceptable only if it fits in with a self-consistent set of propositions about how things in the world really are.

Of course, the neo-rationalist recognizes the truth of Ryle's observation that much practical activity appears to happen automatically and immediately, without the actor having to stop and think. But such activity, along with the judgments upon which it is based, is nonetheless thought necessarily to presuppose, and to activate, an often immense structure of propositional commitment that is implicit and that, as such, composes the strongly intellectual, if only tacit, underpinnings of the action itself, hence of the judgment that it embodies. As we have seen, a rich structure of implicit, immediate and deeply engaged (non-detached) belief is perfectly consistent with a highly intellectualistic understanding of action and judgment, and some such notion is exactly what the neo-rationalist proposes. The argument also presumes, however, that implicit beliefs can, in principle, be made explicit. Specifically, an intellectualist/rationalist account of action and judgment contemplates the ever-present possibility of what may be called "rational reconstruction." What makes action and judgment intelligible and meaningful – what distinguishes it, for example, from the behavior of animals or, perhaps, machines – is that it is always eligible for some kind of systematic post-hoc analysis in which implicit, unstated, tacit assumptions and linkages can be uncovered, explored, and evaluated. Practical judgment and action is understood, thereby, as a kind of intelligent performance.

Even the simple and seemingly autonomic act of opening a door in fact reflects an immense array of beliefs or truth claims that the actor has absorbed and to which he or she is committed, even if only tacitly, and that can easily be made explicit if the circumstances so require. Just as I know, as a propositional or intellectual matter, that a violin is smaller than the Atlantic Ocean, so does the skillful and highly practiced opener of doors know very well what doors and doorknobs are and at least roughly how they work. Again, one test of this is to imagine posing hypothetical questions of that individual – questions about the structure and function of doors and doorknobs; and there seems little doubt that such questions would generally be answered immediately, even instantly, and with great accuracy.

The neo-rationalist claims, finally, that specifically political judgment proceeds very much in this way. Political actions reflect judgments that, in turn, reflect propositions or truth claims pertaining, typically, to those public policies that are best suited to achieving the goals of the political system, such as they may be. Political judgments are, therefore, fully eligible for rational reconstruction; and such reconstruction is apt to ask of any particular political claim – whether implicit or otherwise – if it is consistent with the larger body of presuppositions to which the culture in question is committed. In this sense, political discourse is, in no small measure, a highly intellectualistic and cognitively rich enterprise in which the cogency of any particular political position becomes, and should become, a topic for explication, analysis, and rational evaluation.

Such a view may in fact be implicit but unrecognized in at least some of the other approaches that we have considered. For example, we have seen how Oakeshott claims that political wisdom emerges out of a certain "mental fog." But in defending himself against critics who contend that his theory disparages the very idea of argumentation in politics, he insists, rightly in my opinion, that his position in fact puts argumentation at the very center of things insofar as the pursuit of intimations requires the political actor to show explicitly how his or her preferred course of action is consistent with or entailed by the predispositions of the relevant culture. Surely any such demonstration – a demonstration of coherence – would necessarily consist of a rational argument of some kind. Thus, when Oakeshott criticizes rationalism in politics, it is actually a very narrow and restricted type of rationalism that he has in mind. His overall view is, in fact, profoundly rationalistic.

In the real world of politics, perhaps the clearest confirmation of neo-rationalist theory is routinely to be found in the written opinions of the United States Supreme Court. Such opinions are explicitly designed to show how – to prove that – a particular decision is (or isn't) consistent with or entailed by the Constitution and the fundamental principles of right and wrong out of which the Constitution emerges. The goal, again, is coherence, and the method is rational. I would suggest, further, that this is only an especially clear case of the policy process more generally conceived. As a rule, policy proposals are presented in the context of supporting evidence and argument designed to show why those proposals should be adopted. Such evidence and argument is always eligible for analysis and evaluation; and the process of analysis and evaluation is, I would suggest, a defining and necessary feature of the political process itself. It is certainly not the entirety of the political process – politics involves power and influence, conflict and interest, coercion and the quest for comparative advantage – but it is precisely the part that focuses on questions of political judgment, very much as the neo-rationalist suggests.

Here, then, is a perspective on political judgment that seeks to retain something like a Platonic emphasis on proof and demonstration – on the mental or intellectual faculty of logical/rational analysis – while at the same time acknowledging both post-Kantian insights into the constructed nature of human knowledge and post-Heideggerian themes regarding the reflexive aspect of practical endeavor. It seeks, in short, to develop a comprehensive account of judgment that brings together any number of seemingly incompatible strands. Whether or not it does so successfully is, of course, a matter for readers to explore in greater detail.

8

The frequent references that I have made throughout this book to Plato and Aristotle, including references that appear in some of the later sections, may give readers the sinking feeling that little progress has been made over the last two and half millennia regarding the question of political judgment. Indeed, the basic problematics involving both the Platonic distinction between knack and craft and the Aristotelian distinction between *phronēsis* and *sophia* seem still to be very much with us today. Are we then no closer to resolving those problematics than were the ancients? Has the venerable tradition of Western philosophical speculation about judgment been barren – a kind of extended, intricate, and tortuous failure? If the questions posed by Plato and Aristotle remain unresolved, does this mean there have been no real advances to speak of?

There are at least three things to be said about this. On the one hand, the persistence of philosophical problems over time is hardly unique to the issue of political judgment. Very basic and seemingly elementary questions about, among many other things, the relationship between mind and body, the possible scope and limits of human knowledge, morality and the freedom of the will, the origins of the world, and the explanation of evil have occasioned lively, on-going, and persistent controversy – both among professional philosophers and within ordinary human discourse – for centuries upon centuries, with no apparent end in sight. Surely the problem of judgment is simply part and parcel of the general pattern. There are, moreover, good reasons for this. We might say that systematic philosophical speculation is nothing less than the attempt to tackle and understand enduring issues that are not enduring by accident, but are endemically so. It is not just that such issues are difficult. Rather, it seems that they are so constructed as inherently to resist final and definitive resolution; they become objects of unusually intense and vigorous speculation precisely because rock-solid answers are and perhaps must be elusive. In this regard, moreover, it is not clear that science itself is all that different. It is obviously – trivially – true that the development of science and technology over time has enabled us to do a virtually infinite number of amazing things that couldn't even be imagined as recently as fifty or a hundred years ago, much less twenty-five hundred years ago. But the success of the scientific enterprise, however astonishing and enormous, nonetheless seems often to rest upon large structures of basic explanation – a "force" such as gravity might be one example – that are essentially postulated as extremely useful and productive imaginings but that are not in themselves well understood. I am suggesting that something roughly analogous might be true for the kind of conceptual analysis that composes the heart of the philosophical enterprise, of a sort that has been outlined in this book.

But second, the persistence of hard questions is perfectly consistent with the possibility that our understanding of those questions – our purchase on the full range of complexities inherent in them – is in fact rather greater than in the past. Indeed, I would suggest that the ideas of Kant and Arendt, and of the many theorists who have embraced or rejected their work, have deepened and enriched our understanding of the problem of judgment in powerful and compelling ways. The tradition of speculation about political judgment has given us an ever more robust and penetrating conceptual apparatus – intellectual tools – for thinking about and making sense of the relevant questions, even if it hasn't (yet) produced final answers. The Kantian distinction between determinate and reflective judgment is only one example of this; and the result is that Platonic/Aristotelian problematics persist, if indeed they do persist, only in sharply reconfigured terms that enable us to acknowledge and work through aspects and implications that had previously remained tacit at best.

But finally, I myself am not at all convinced that a neo-rationalist account of a kind that I have sketched in the present chapter doesn't point the way toward arriving at answers that might in fact prove to be satisfying, persuasive and sound in the long run. Such answers might indeed count – collectively – as an updated form of Platonism. But I think such a form of Platonism would be virtually unrecognizable to Plato himself, based as it would be on new conceptions of rationality as well as on a sharper understanding of both the strengths and weaknesses of the anti-rationalist perspective, as that approach has been formulated and reformulated over time.

In my view, philosophical endeavor – including political philosophy – is a matter of making our implicit conceptual and metaphysical commitments explicit, of unearthing and explicating foundational intuitions and allowing them, thereby, to be the subject of self-conscious critical engagement and revision. It is a matter, in short, of thought thinking itself. It would be no wonder, then, that foundational works of antiquity would continue to demand our attention, since they stand at or near the genealogical roots of our shared if often unstated understanding of how things in the world really are. With this in mind, moreover, one might say that the topic of judgment – political or otherwise – would actually seem to play a special role, since our discovery and assessment of underlying metaphysical/conceptual claims can itself only be a matter of judgment. The enterprise is, in effect, not simply a matter of thought thinking itself but of making judgments about judgments, and doing so in a way that avoids vicious circularity by seeking and, in the best possible circumstance, finding formulations that uniquely pass the test of consistency – the test of making sense – and that stand, at least for us, as answers that must be accepted on pain of incoherence. From such a perspective, the continued pursuit of philosophical problems, including the problem of political judgment, is an on-going, necessary, open-ended, and uplifting endeavor, an important part of what makes us human. It is a pursuit that I have tried to follow in this book, and it is one that I recommend to my readers with considerable enthusiasm.

Notes

Introduction

1 David Brooks, "The C. E. O. in Politics," *New York Times* (January 12, 2012).
2 Considerations of ordinary language usage may create a certain ambiguity here. Obviously, our concern is with the analysis of good judgment, as opposed to simply judgment. But when we say of someone that he or she is "a person of judgment," this often or usually implies, in and of itself, that he or she is a person of good judgment. At times, then, I will talk about "judgment" and at other times specifically about "good judgment," and hopefully the context will make clear when and if I think the modifier is superfluous. Sometimes it will be and sometimes it won't.
3 Robert E. Rubin, "America's Bank," *New York Times Sunday Book Review* (October 19, 2015), p. 1.

Chapter 1 Foundations: Plato and Aristotle

1 For the full discussion, see Plato, *Gorgias* 449a–462b.
2 Plato, *Gorgias* 462c.
3 Plato, *Republic* 473b.
4 Plato, *Republic* 473d.
5 Plato, *Gorgias* 454c.
6 Plato, *Republic* 489a–495a.

Chapter 2 The Kantian Problematic

1 My account of Plato focuses on so-called middle period works, primarily the *Republic* and also the *Gorgias*. But somewhat later works, such as the *Statesman* or, arguably, the *Laws* might suggest that Plato's views changed or, perhaps, were more complicated and varied than I have indicated. (The *Statesman* [294b–c], for example, may be thought to anticipate something like Aristotle's account of *phronēsis* with respect, in particular, to the application of general laws to particular cases.) This, however, is not the place to work through the finer points of Plato interpretation; and what I've had to say is certainly an accurate account of Plato's most influential writing on politics.

2 Aristotle, *Nicomachean Ethics*, 1141b25–35.

3 Aristotle, *Nicomachean Ethics*, 1141b25–1142a30.

4 As a historical matter, the tradition rarely considered the possibility of women in leadership roles.

5 Thucydides, *The Peloponnesian War* (Indianapolis: Hackett, 1998 [410 BCE?]), Section 138.

6 Cicero, *On the Commonwealth* (New York: Macmillan, 1976), p. 139.

7 Tacitus, *The Agricola and the Germania* (London: Penguin, 1970), pp. 54–9.

8 For a representative text, see James VI and I, "The Trew Law of Free Monarchies," in David Wootton et al., *Divine Right and Democracy: An Anthology of Political Writings in Stuart England* (New York: Penguin, 1988).

9 See for example, Francesco Guicciardini, *Maxims and Reflections of a Renaissance Statesman* (New York: Harper and Row, 1965), and Niccolo Machiavelli, *The Prince* (New York: W. W. Norton, 1977).

10 Polybius, *The Histories* (Oxford: Oxford University Press, 2010), p. 372.

11 Alexander Hamilton, James Madison and John Jay, *The Federalist Papers* (New York: Signet Classics, 1999), p. 319.

12 Thomas Hobbes, *Leviathan*, Book I, Chapters 8–9.

13 For a discussion, see Peter J. Steinberger, "Hobbesian Resistance," *American Journal of Political Science* 46:4 (October 2002).

14 The *locus classicus* is Immanuel Kant, *The Critique of Judgment* (New York: Hafner Press, 1951 [1790]).

Chapter 3 The Arendtian Theory of Judgment

1 Hannah Arendt, *The Human Condition* (Chicago: University of Chicago Press, 1958).
2 See Hannah Arendt, "Thinking and Moral Considerations," *Social Research* 38 (1971), pp. 430–48. For my own view, see Peter J. Steinberger, "Hannah Arendt on Judgment," *American Journal of Political Science* 34:3 (August 1990).
3 Ronald Beiner, *Political Judgment* (Chicago: University of Chicago Press, 1983).
4 Hannah Arendt, *Lectures on Kant's Political Philosophy* (Chicago: University of Chicago Press, 1982).
5 Beiner, *Political Judgment*, p. 131.
6 Linda Zerilli, *A Democratic Theory of Judgment* (Chicago: University of Chicago Press, 2016). For related arguments, see Kennan Ferguson, *The Politics of Judgment: Aesthetics, Identity, and Political Theory* (Lanham, Maryland: Lexington Books, 1999), which proposes a largely aesthetic account of judgment and Albena Azmanova, *The Scandal of Reason: A Critical Theory of Political Judgment* (New York: Columbia University Press, 2012), which focuses on processes of moral discourse and deliberation.
7 Zerilli, *A Democratic Theory of Judgment*, p. 9.
8 Zerilli, *A Democratic Theory of Judgment*, p. 271.
9 Ruth Leys, "The Turn to Affect: A Critique," *Critical Inquiry* 37:3 (2011), p. 437.

Chapter 4 Hermeneutics, Tacit Knowledge, and Neo-Rationalism

1 The principal text is Hans-Georg Gadamer, *Truth and Method* (New York: Crossroads Press, 1989), originally published in German in 1960.
2 Plato, *Meno* (80D).
3 Michael Oakeshott, *Rationalism in Politics and Other Essays* (London: Methuen, 1962). Particularly recommended for our purposes are the title essay and the essay on "Political Education." For a discussion of Oakeshott and Gadamer, see Edmund Neill, "Michael Oakeshott and Hans-Georg Gadamer on Practices, Social Science, and Modernity," *History of European Ideas* 40:3 (2014).

4   Michael Oakeshott, *Experience and its Modes* (Cambridge: Cambridge University Press, 1985 [1933]), p. 321.

5   Edward H. Levi, *An Introduction to Legal Reasoning* (Chicago: University of Chicago Press, 1949).

6   Stanley Fish, *Is There a Text in this Class?* (Cambridge: Harvard University Press, 1982).

7   Ronald Dworkin, "How Law is Like Literature," in *A Matter of Principle* (Cambridge: Harvard University Press, 1985).

8   Stanley Fish, "Working on the Chain Gang: Interpretation in the Law and in Literary Criticism" *Critical Inquiry* 9 (September 1982).

9   Alessandro Ferrara, *Justice and Judgment: The Rise and Prospect of the Judgment Model in Contemporary Political Philosophy* (London: Sage Publications, 1999), p. 5. Ferrara is here quoting the influential Italian philosopher Luigi Pareyson.

10 Alessandro Ferrara, *The Force of the Example: Explorations in the Paradigm of Judgment* (New York: Columbia University Press, 2008), p. 31.

11 I ignore here a third way in which an individual can be said to know something, namely, knowledge by acquaintance – as in Susan "knows" (is acquainted with) Mary.

12 For a discussion, see Leslie Paul Thiele, *The Heart of Judgment: Practical Wisdom, Neuroscience, and Narrative* (Cambridge: Cambridge University Press, 2006).

13 See Peter J. Steinberger, *The Concept of Political Judgment* (Chicago: University of Chicago Press, 1993); and Peter J. Steinberger, "Rationalism in Politics," *American Political Science Review* 109:4 (November 2015).

Index